FESTIVALS & RITUALS OF SPAIN

FESTIVALS & RITUALS OF SPAIN

Cristina García Rodero

Text by J. M. Caballero Bonald

HARRY N. ABRAMS, INC., PUBLISHERS

Translated from the Spanish by Wayne Finke

Editor, English-language edition: Lory Frankel

Library of Congress Cataloging-in-Publication Data

García Rodero, Cristina, 1949–
Festivals and rituals of Spain / photographs by Cristina García Rodero ;
text by J. M. Caballero Bonald.
p.   cm.
ISBN 0–8109–3839–1
1. Festivals—Spain. 2. Festivals—Spain—Pictorial works. 3. Spain—Social
life and customs. 4. Spain—Social life and customs—Pictorial works.
I. Caballero Bonald, José Manuel, 1926–. II. Title.
GT4862.A2G37   1994
394.2′6946—dc20   93–23289

Published in 1994 by Harry N. Abrams, Incorporated, New York
A Times Mirror Company

Printed and bound in Spain

CONTENTS

FOREWORD

Since 1973 Cristina García Rodero has devoted all her free time and resources to a single-minded quest for images that capture the pathos, complexity, vigor, and beauty of the towns and people of Spain in the exceptional and fleeting moments when it is on festive display. García Rodero has made some fifteen hundred visits to festivals which she discovered by going from town to town. Her work, mostly carried out single-handedly, has been made more congenial thanks to an informal network of friends, including journalists, photographers, and her own family members, who have at times accompanied her on her journeys.

García Rodero's vision is very personal. She observes those moments when the public mask and the private face intersect and the extraordinary and the routine are juxtaposed, avoiding festivals too finished and formal. Cristina waits patiently for the unexpected, the unforeseen: the hooded penitent who suddenly, inspired, takes an acrobatic leap into the air. She has an open, direct sympathy with the rural people who still know how to laugh, cry, pray, express wonderment, or rejoice in the streets. The result is a document of the human condition, seen in instances of special intensity produced by the annual cycle of festivals.

García Rodero's well-organized photographic archive is an invaluable resource for the history, culture, and art of the towns and villages of Spain. Its immense value has been recognized, in particular by the Getty Center for the History of Art and the Humanities in Santa Monica, California, which holds some six thousand photographs catalogued for consultation by the public. The towns photographed will discover here in this archive a vast treasure for future generations.

In a certain sense, Cristina has succeeded in creating her own geography of Spain's special places, as she has highlighted towns and villages unknown to people from the city. Year after year she returns to places like Acehúche, Albalá, Almonacid del Marquesado, Almonte, Amil, Bercianos de Aliste, Berga, Camuñas, Castrillo de Murcia, Ciudadela, El Cerro de Andévalo, Forcall, Garganta la Olla, Gende, Ituren, Laza, Lequeitio, Lorca, Lumbier, Montamarta, Morella, Peñalsordo, Peñas de San Pedro, Puebla de Guzmán, Puente Genil, Ribarteme, Riofrío de Aliste, Saavedra, San Pedro Manrique, San Vicente de la Sonsierra, Sanzoles, Useres, Yebra de Basa, and Zarza de Montánchez — almost mythical names for her and those who love her photographs. In many towns like these she is recognized and welcomed by dancers, mayordomos or mayordomas, priests, mayors, and civil guards, her best sources of information. She celebrates her reencounters with pilgrims, drummers, photographers, traders, itinerant ice cream sellers, and professional beggars who — like she — form part of the festival. Welcome, then, fellow reader, to this galaxy of special places whose inhabitants, with their festivals, excel in creating a time outside of time and sharing it with others.

In these photographs you will discover two types of art. One is the tenacious, sensitive, quick-witted art of García Rodero expressed in the way she has obtained, composed, and selected these images. The other is the anonymous, ephemeral art to which she renders homage: that of the men and women, boys and girls who decorate their streets with papers, flowers, and branches. They arrange the streetside altars for Corpus Christi with images, jars, and bedspreads. They prepare artistically designed breads and pastry rings as offerings. For the processions they embroider banners and cloaks to be placed on the images. They sew traditional costumes for the dancers and invent fantastic garb and masks or carefully reconstruct old masks for Carnival. They adorn their horses with papers, flowers, bows, and blankets. For weeks and even months they work in secret to dazzle spectators with resplendent crosses in May or sculptures to be consumed on the bonfires. When you contemplate these photographs, imagine yourself there, in the festival, your senses awakened. These images contain the fragrance of roses and choking smoke, the booming of guns, insistent drumbeats, the slightly off-key music of the municipal band, the murmured reciting of the rosary, spirited declamations in verse, singing, jeering, vivas, and the neighing of a frightened horse.

William A. Christian, Jr.

INTRODUCTION

Cristina García Rodero has over twenty long years traversed the hidden, complex, multiform roads of Spain. She carried no other baggage than her camera, apart from — naturally — an indefatigable artistic drive and a fervent, expert curiosity. Thus she journeyed more than three hundred and fifty thousand miles and collected everything that had to do with festivals, beliefs, rituals, and traditions in Spain's mainland and island towns and cities. The result has been dazzlingly effective. I am inclined to believe that never until now has a graphic document of such aesthetically impeccable and culturally rigorous material been amassed. It actually constitutes a useful and extremely beautiful anthropological archive whose value will even increase as time snatches some of these treasures of local customs away from us.

It is undeniable that Spanish festivals, or the most integral individual ceremonies that compose them, have sustained marked alterations with the passage of time. Of course, this is something that always happens. All artistic expression — even that of a popular nature — normally undergoes a series of evolving processes and even one crisis of identity or another, obeying the natural progression of life and the very dynamism of history. But renovation from within is one thing and deliberate deformation quite another. Provided it is owed to the whims of frivolity or the artifice of fashion, almost any change can be legitimate. There are those who believe that the best way to remain faithful to a tradition is to modernize the most useful elements of that tradition. However, this supposition calls for clarification. If one understands by tradition the genuine manner of the transmission of certain facts and beliefs through time, it is clear that any attempt to engineer that legacy carries with it the danger of adulteration. But if the idea is to adapt certain traditions, rejuvenating them in one way or another to preserve them from any presumed risk of extinction, such an attitude will always be defendable.

The majority of ethnographers and folklorists are convinced that the profound changes in the modes of urban and rural life occasioned in the last decades have also brought about a slow impoverishment, or at least a certain vitiation of popular festivals. This seems plausible if one focuses on the role of the younger generation, which habitually rejects age-old local customs it finds unappealing or out-of-date. Youthful tastes and pleasures follow other paths. The younger generation's lack of interest has created a hole in the proceedings, as the festival loses something of its most definable essence: serving as a vehicle for interchange among a whole town's citizenry. No festive ritual holds meaning without the participation — active or passive — of the entire community that celebrates it.

Of course, one could also postulate the opposite. There are towns that have succeeded in rescuing in recent times many venerable traditions — dances, songs, costumes, usages, and time-immemorial rituals — of which scarcely any traces remained, as if it were a matter of instinctively recovering a personality. The examples are legion. However, it may be that the critical undertaking of removing the dust from certain popular festivals — irrespective of the narrow goals of those with an eye on the tourist trade — has occasionally led to a subversive tendency to "reinvent" tradition. However, considering the potential for irrevocable loss, this sometimes hasty push for restoration can be justified, since in the long run something will have been saved from oblivion.

The photographs collected here comprise a master inventory of local customs in a better or worse state of preservation. The book suffers, however, from a deficiency I cannot neglect to point out. This is that Cristina García Rodero herself was not the one to write the short but passionate story of each and every one of the photographic documents that appear in this work. It was she who explored, photographed, and selected the marvelous fragments of life documented in these pages. It would have been fitting for her to offer commentary on that magnificent fieldwork carried out by someone who, besides being an extraordinary photographer, is also an experienced specialist in the cultural study of Spanish popular festivals. Failing to convince her to take on such a complementary enrichment of the volume, it falls to me to attempt to express what she would have elucidated so magnificently.

Thus, not wishing to impose my point of view on Cristina García Rodero's work, the following text does not consist of specific notes to the photographs. Instead, I have limited myself to sketching a general picture of the most notable Spanish popular festivals, adding only some spontaneous reflective thought and conclusions of a personal nature. Naturally, I am the inevitable beneficiary of guides written by those who have better studied and classified the historical and cultural terrain of these festivals, notably the distinguished scholar Julio Caro Baroja.

SPANISH FESTIVAL CYCLES

The folkloric heritage of a people amounts to the ultimate outcome of a long process of cultural revisions. It is safe to suppose that the collective acceptance of a specific repertory of usages and customs, apart from the unconscious mechanisms of inheritance, comes about through a sort of crystallization of very different elements following one another in time. These are assimilated by fashion and embraced by the popular imagination. From this point of view, it is not unusual for a festival to evolve with the same rhythm as its participants. Each locality is subject to different types of new stimuli that modify, for better or worse, the many age-old festival practices. Among the most common sources of changes are private interests in the community or commercial incentives of a social group that have altered the celebration of a festival in favor of a more spectacular display in order to satisfy the demands of tourism. In some cases, they have added only superficial decorations, but in others they have systematically weakened and diluted the nature of the celebration. Their effect has depended on local influences and obligations.

The roots of the great majority of Spanish popular festivals — and, in general, all Western festivals — apparently are hidden in the shadowy realm of ancient nature cults, which were affected successively by history and enclosed in legend, which is sometimes a disguised version of history. But in this area, one must proceed with great caution. To refer to ancestral rituals, usages, and beliefs as deriving from the most remote bases of popular culture is always risky, if not erroneous. One may glimpse traces of archaic significance, scarcely recognizable, in the background of a particular festivity, but all such presumed survivals are always highly debatable.

Suffice it to say that the practices peculiar to a popular festival have suffered abundant modification, in general due to the corruption of their transmission, the historical ebb and flow, and even religious conventions. From the beginning, the Church sought, with astuteness and diligence, to counteract the evident pagan marks of many festivals by readapting them to its liturgy. That is, rather than prohibiting them it adopted them, thus successfully gaining the people's voluntary acceptance of a type of reconversion that incidentally quashed certain superstitions and doctrinal errors. According to Blanco White, "our ancient ecclesiastical festivals were created as substitutes for the pagan rites that Christian priests could not eradicate by other means." In this way, the liturgical year prevailed over the pagan calendar of festivals, and that religious strategy affected the repertory of nonreligious customs.

The body of a people's festival traditions can be classified very differently, according to the ways in which they influence the lives of their participants or the period of time when they are held. Festivals develop — or were born — in intimate relationship with the changes of nature and the human particularities of urban or rural areas. Each popular celebration has had — and may continue to have — a relevant link with the special events, religious or secular, of its community. Apart from the direct influence of the weather on the produce of the earth, a summer festival will never arise from the same human reasons as a winter festival, nor one in the shadowy mountain ranges as one held on the sunny coast. It also will not follow the same path of cultural transmission. Local or regional history is a decisive factor here. Even given a wellspring of very similar general principles to account for the origins of festivals, in the long run it is the nature and rhythm of the particular idiosyncrasy that matter. Between an Andalusian and a Galician pilgrimage, for example, or a Holy Week in either Zamora or Murcia, or a carnival in Tenerife or the Basque country, we find identical causes but very different effects.

It is easiest, as well as customary, to establish four basic Spanish festival cycles, in more or less direct relationship with the course of the seasons.

For these purposes, however, it is important not to impose rigid boundaries on them, for they commonly overlap. Within these cycles — spring, summer, autumn, winter — lies a very diverse group of traditional festivals, rituals, and beliefs of varying nature. What distinguishes one from another is how they reflect time's flow, how they respond to the basic phases of their community's development. In a general way, spring and summer festivities, apart from their religious associations, arise from elements related to agriculture — planting, harvesting, prayers for rain or for fair weather, blessing of the fields, ritual practices related to the earth's fecundity or inactivity. Those held in autumn are fewer in number and normally less exultant, and those celebrated in winter tend to be dramatic and ceremonial.

Whether the warm season ebbs, to be replaced by cold and snow, or the signs of nature's reawakening begin to appear, festivals and the people promoting them shift their habits and ways. By looking at the Christian calendar — Easter Sunday, Pentecost, Corpus Christi, the Assumption, Advent, Christmas, Epiphany, Carnival, Lent, Holy Week, and so on, without forgetting the saints' days — the chronology of Spanish festivals can be followed very precisely over the course of a year. But to this and other curiosities of local customs we shall devote the following pages.

SPRING FESTIVALS

With the rebirth of the earth and the first hints of good weather, there begins a series of festivals that exhibit clearly distinctive elements, even when they are considered as the fruit of the festivals that preceded them or as sowing the seeds of those that follow. One might say that the rituals in honor of the sun begin to replace those of the night. As the countryside grows green and flowers bud in springtime, life also begins again symbolically. Many age-old variations of the cult of love, life's supreme reference point, now realize their most propitious moments for making their appearance. In the regions where spring comes early, Andalusia, lower Extremadura, Murcia, Valencia, the desire for festivals seems to heighten — assuming that this desire had languished during the rest of the year. The people expand in the warm weather and think about enjoying their leisure collectively. Life, once again, adjusts to the rhythm of nature; the traces of agrarian culture, intermingled with practices of a religious character, generally interposed in a subtle manner, reappear in a goodly number of spring festivals: pilgrimages, maypole celebrations, fairs, and floral decorations for doorways and balconies.

As is common in rituals dedicated to the sun, the diverse ceremonies revolving around fire play a significant role throughout this cycle of traditional celebrations. Between the vernal equinox and the summer solstice, two moments greatly charged with symbolism in the calendar of Western festivals — that is, between Saint Joseph's Day, or March 19, and Saint John's Day, June 24, in the liturgical calendar — many Mediterranean peoples pay homage to the sun, represented by fire, with practices of magic or purification, merriment or devotion. In addition to fire, the natural world — the green land, the promise of the harvest, the tree with its many cultural associations, all heralding the earth's fertility and procreation — assumes its most eloquent allegorical form in the course of spring festivals.

Here the line between winter and spring blurs, for many festivals still related to the liturgical cycle of winter — as, for example, Holy Week — already contain the seed of an authentic spring celebration in southern latitudes. The same could be said of the May festivals, which have much in common with summer festivals. Besides, it is a well-known fact that the Christian calendar, adapted to the lunar calendar, requires Easter Sunday — the axis for that unfurling series of liturgical festivals — to be fixed on the Sunday following the first full moon after the vernal equinox, while the dates for celebrating many festivities, from Carnival to Pentecost, are quite movable. Holy Week can be commemorated just before the vernal equinox or very late in April. In any case, a clear-cut cyclical division of festivals according to the season when they are celebrated is not particularly essential. Pilgrimages and fairs, for example, while largely springtime phenomena, occur until the cold weather of autumn arrives.

Fallas and Flower Festivals

Around Saint Joseph's Day, just before the vernal equinox, Valencia's streets teem with a procession of *ninots*, or figures, destined to be consumed in the immense *falla*, or bonfire, of a fantastic sacrifice, once the figures' mission as witnesses is fulfilled. Local artisans, equipped with exquisite tools from the Baroque period, labor all year to create and model these figures, which take on some relevant aspect of local or national politics, a phenomenon of many other places and festive occasions as well. Such ingenuity joined with a critical faculty transforms the *fallas* into a journalistic showcase on a monumental scale. Almost all the remaining elements of the spectacle — costumes, music, processions, and banquets — are mere decorations embellishing the solar significance of an eminently Mediterranean festival not without its complexities. No doubt the successive ritual of games, including fireworks, focuses the symbolism of the *fallas*. The bonfires crackle with the same rough language as the rockets, and a progression of musical bands and the cries of the crowd add modern elements to the splendid, primal ceremony of fire.

Some have sought to discover the origin of these bonfires of Saint Joseph's Day in the figures and puppets that burn so profusely in other very different places and occasions: Christmas, Carnival, Lent, Easter Sunday, to name a few. In Valencia, too, the ritual of the *fallas* clearly serves as a cleansing process, an antidote, and, simultaneously, a purification rite against the shadows of life that the bonfires undertake to dissipate. Is winter thus bade farewell or is spring thus welcomed? It matters little. Perhaps both purposes are joined in the metaphoric realm of fire.

The spring cycle of festivals is also profusely represented by allegories of the natural world. It is not necessary to repeat here the extent to which the vestiges of agrarian culture persist in many of these popular celebrations succeeding each other with the same rhythm as spring's regenerative saps. In these festivals, the collective nostalgia for all that so-often-lost splendor of nature, for times when the woods and forests formed the daily landscape for the people, emerges. The tree, venerated in different ways in the four corners of the globe, has since prehistoric times gained a cult following that, through the natural circumstances of spring, coincides with the rituals of love. The garlands and maypole celebrations mentioned here are but extensions of those first festivals in which love seems to become infected with the promising prodigality of nature.

The celebrations known as flower festivals — a name also for the songs traditionally performed on such occasions — preferably begin in Castile-León and upper Extremadura, perhaps on account of the contrasts of weather. Relating with unchanging meaning to the seasonal agricultural labors, they do not fail to embrace one of the already mentioned and most pronounced characteristics of spring: love, here centered on the folkloric customs of courtship and marriage, and, in no small measure, a veiled erotic impulse. Traditional practices such as youths strolling around town, courting the young girls with serenades, and serenades before the homes of the best man and bridesmaid on the eve of a wedding combine with other truly peasant rituals. The banners of floral garlands, the decorations of leaves and ribbons on the top of a pole carried on these occasions by farmers on returning from their daily labors are perhaps but vestiges of ancient initiation rites centered on the earth's fertility. This is not, of course, exclusive to the flower festivals of Extremadura and Castile-León.

In Talavera de la Reina, for example, a well-known festival called the Día de las Mondas (Day of the Prunings) is celebrated on Easter Saturday (it was originally held on Easter Tuesday). Its ceremony is no doubt associated with the centuries-old cult of Ceres, the Roman goddess of agriculture (Demeter in ancient Greek mythology). This unusual semipagan, semireligious festival, nearly forgotten for decades, has been resurrected, especially its costumes, offerings, and dances, as is also happening with other April festivities linked to the awakening of nature and the sacred mythology of fertility. Another such festival is the Bando de la Huerta (Blessing of the Orchard) of Murcia, with its *entierro de la sardina*, or burial of the sardine. Here, apart from the late echo of Carnival, symbolic homage is rendered to the yearly gifts of mother earth.

Holy Week

We have already noted that Holy Week, as a movable ecclesiastical festival, can in certain places constitute a type of additional prelude to spring. In Andalusia and Murcia, already at the end of March or in mid-April, around Palm Sunday, the climate traditionally possesses not only liturgical but also floral connotations. The smell of wax from candles burning on the floats is mixed with the fragrance of orange blossom. And on those austere and penitential days evoking the Passion of Christ, it is a perennial delight to witness nature's sensual collaboration in helping to make the Holy Week of Andalusia or Murcia an eminently springtime festival.

The festive customs accompanying Holy Week differ substantially from one region to another. Although the religious wellsprings are of course the same, their forms of appearance depend directly on local characteristics. Such a conclusion seems obvious when observing the very marked differences between an Andalusian Holy Week and one in Castile. Just to cite two extreme examples, Seville and Valladolid represent in this sense two opposing poles of religiousness. While the Andalusian capital emphasizes exaltation, heterodox vitality, a flood of sensual decorations, the Castilian capital admits nothing apart from devotion, austerity, liturgical orthodoxy. Neither do the processions of the religious brotherhoods or the attitudes of the people coincide. In Castile or in the northern part of the peninsula, people attend processions as if it were a Stations of the Cross in the interior of a church; in Andalusia the participants escorting the floats share an outward enthusiasm and festive spirit that might even strike one as contradictory. It is as though the Andalusian were already conscious of the triumphant epilogue of the Resurrection and preferred to temper the holy drama of the Passion with a type of anticipatory and heightened rejoicing. In any case, the religious, social, and cultural circumstances that come together in the Holy Week par excellence are extremely complex, as exemplified by Seville.

There is no doubt that the *hiperdulía* cult — that is, of the Holy Virgin — is linked to ancient Mediterranean religious practices. In Andalusia this cult takes on a genuine and unique expression. These floats of the Virgin with faces of beautiful, afflicted women, floats adorned to an extreme with all manner of baroque attributes, are treated, quite unabashedly, as human entities. Rocked by the *costaleros*, or float carriers, perhaps to accentuate the

feminine condition, the Virgins, whose central role displaces that of the Christ figures, are exalted jubilantly through the streets, even flirted at with a metaphorical ingenuity that might strike one as most irreverent. Even the religious brotherhoods, many of them having their roots in ancient guilds, compete in luxury, street displays, and partisan excesses through their strange domestic statutes and inherited fervor. The penitences and rigors proper to the period are relegated to other social realms.

There is a great variety of practices linked to Holy Week. Among the peculiarities of local traditions can be found the jointed Christ figures who bless the fields in Arcos de la Frontera (Cádiz) and Tobarra (Albacete) or imitate scenes of the Passion in Ocaña and Peraleda de la Mata (Toledo). Then there are the spectacular and almost carnivalesque rivalries of the *blancos y azules* (whites and blues) of Lorca (Murcia); the terrible self-infliction of the *empalaos* (impaled) of Valverde de la Vera (Cáceres) or of the *picaos* (pierced) of San Vicente de la Sonsierra (La Rioja); the bizarre and bloody *tamborradas* (drumrolls) of Calanda, Híjar, and Alcañiz (Teruel), Baena (Córdoba) or Hellín (Albacete); the stagings of the Passion in various Catalonian localities, including Esparraguera and Olesa de Montserrat (Barcelona), Vergès (Gerona), Cervera (Lérida), and in other towns of Castile, Asturias, the Basque country, and the Valencia region.

Pilgrimages and Fairs

Beginning with the liturgical summit of Easter Sunday, Spaniards tend to go out into the countryside. After the celebrations of the "encounter" of the resurrected Christ with his Mother and the burning or destruction of numerous types of figures or puppets representing Judas, the period propitious for blessing the fields, requesting positive intervention of the Virgin and saints, relaxing in areas beside hermitages, and practicing cults related to the vivifying waters begins in earnest. The pagan foundation of these beliefs, which are linked to the cult of Ceres or to agriculture in general, was joined to similar ecclesiastical festivals, as occured in the great majority of cases. Many beliefs in supernatural forces and many prophetic and healing rituals were fused with the compact nucleus of prayer, blessings, and country festivities beside sanctuaries of highly esteemed devotion. Thus begins the joyful cycle of pilgrimages, a cycle that will not really end until summer's decline and even autumn's first harbingers.

To prepare a catalogue of these Spanish pilgrimages would be an arduous if not limitless task. The processions of Virgins or more or less miraculous saints can be discovered in any corner of Spain. Each one assimilates into its character the generalized pious tradition, adding or taking away clearly local elements. Very few towns renounce the opportunity to get out into the countryside when it begins to form an enjoyable setting for relaxation and the demonstration of faith. Religious practices no doubt compose the essential basis for these festivities, although their visible forms are of a very different essence, depending on how religious fervor and merriment are combined.

There are those who go on a pilgrimage accompanied by a sincere devotion to the Virgin or the particular saint venerated in their town, and there are those who use that devotion as a mere pretext for rejoicing. Neither of the two motives is incompatible; they are, in fact, interchangeable. It often happens that religious sentiment infects the most indifferent and unifies all the pilgrims in one and the same confraternity, without distinction in attitudes. Even doubters, given a readily accessible festive spirit, can participate in these celebrations. Faith does not exclude merriment, nor does penitence displace relaxation. It is true that anything can happen on a pilgrimage. The abundance of wine and food, pious exaltation, and the enforced opportunities for social fellowship have more than once corroborated this observation.

Galician pilgrimages are numerous and very suggestive. Although the symbolic universe is no different from that of any similar celebration usually consisting of the age-old symbols of water, the tree, and the stone, the very peculiarities of Galician popular mythology endow these festivities with a special personality. All such festivals claim a holy fountain, a legendary woods, and a sacred stone in the origin of every sanctuary, perhaps even more so in those found in Galicia.

Although they are chronologically situated in the summer cycle, it is pertinent to mention at least two impressive Galician pilgrimages here: the pilgrimage of Santa Marta de Riberteme (Las Nieves, Pontevedra) and that of Puebla de Caramiñal (La Coruña). The first presents a hair-raising procession of coffins occupied by the *ofrecidos* (offered), those who were cured of some grave affliction and now demonstrate their strange form of gratitude to the saint. The pilgrimage of Puebla de Caramiñal, no less frightening, is known as the Procession of the Shrouds. In these and other Galician celebrations, the "holy company" escorts the pilgrims who return to town via shadowy shortcuts through the oak groves. And, according to the proverb recalled by María Angeles Sánchez, one of Spain's most eminent folklorists, "Who did not go as a live person goes as a dead one" on the almost mythical pilgrimage of San Andrés de Teixidó (La Coruña), held in the autumn.

In contrast to these funereal, archaic rituals are, among the innumerable Spanish pilgrimages based on festive excursions to hermitages and sanctuaries, two held in Andalusia that are immensely popular: the pilgrimage of the Virgen del Rocío (Virgin of the Dew) and that of the Virgen de la Cabeza (Virgin of the Head). The first no doubt constitutes an event that goes beyond the limits of cultural anthropology to touch on sociology. It is held on the Pentecost, that is, fifty days after Easter. The village where the sanctuary is located, in the Huelva municipality of Almonte on the banks of the Coto de Doñana, has grown gradually as the number of pilgrims who wished to have a house nearby mushroomed. Hundreds of thousands of persons arrive in Almonte, either in the company of religious brotherhoods or alone, from all corners of the nation.

The village of El Rocío greatly resembles a town in the American West, with its dusty streets, small houses and sheds, and hubbub of horses and carriages. The apotheosis occurs with the procession of the Virgin out of the church. She is forcibly "taken" by the townsfolk, the only persons entrusted with her float, who prevent the uninitiated from drawing too near the procession. This action calls to mind a Dionysian ingredient, which persists in the sacred bases of some religious celebrations. Called White Dove and Star of the Marshlands, the Virgin of El Rocío is a type of Christian substitute for the mother goddess of some of those ancestral cults that also flourished in this Andalusian region, where legend blends miraculously with history. In addition, the colorful masses of people congregating in the El Rocío festivities customarily spend several days engaging in all types of loose behavior, listening feverishly to the sounds of the *sevillanas rocieras* (Sevillian pilgrim girls) or parading on horseback or on foot along the sandy ground marked like streets. Many bring an unbound fervor to the religious ceremonies, and many devote their energies to showing themselves in public and participating in the innumerable private revels.

The pilgrimage of the Virgen de la Cabeza, held on the last Sunday in April, is, on a smaller scale, very similar to that of El Rocío. Cervantes even mentioned it in his last novel, *Los trabajos de Persiles y Sigismunda* of 1617, describing it as very famous and centuries-old. The countryside surrounding the sanctuary — in the jurisdiction of Andújar, by the steep mountain peaks of the Sierra Morena range — is very different from that of El Rocío, although the celebratory customs are not: horse riders, the houses of religious brotherhood, merriment on the road, a multitude of the devout and the revelers in equal portions. The religious ritual unfolds, as usually happens, within the thousand-odd rituals of

the festival. But the common denominator — so proverbially Andalusian — is the exalted cult of the Virgin of miraculous apparition in the cleft of a rock or a tree. Its roots may also be linked to some pre-Christian goddess, the protector of nature.

While it may not constitute a pilgrimage, it seems appropriate to describe here the celebration in Atienza (Guadalajara) of a relevant historical event. It is reputed that the citizens of Atienza valiantly hid the child king Alphonse VIII, saving him from persecution by the Leonese king Ferdinand II, who sought to usurp him from the Castilian throne. The feat took place on Pentecost Sunday, 1163, and since then the aptly named Caballada (Drove of Horses) has been celebrated in this period of spring, with the expected modifications arising from the passage of time. The members of the religious brotherhood of the same name ride their horses through the streets of the town, with the *Manda* (Chief) at the lead, after which they perform the ancient Dance of the Brethren.

The sizable catalogue of fairs also opens at this time, early spring, and, like the pilgrimages, can extend until autumn. Apart from their links to cattle-raising and agriculture, these fairs are not particularly old nor attached to any traditional symbolism. The festivities themselves generally began to take form barely a century ago, probably arising from the excitement of the cattle markets. From a strictly folkloric point of view, they may not fit perfectly in the present inventory, for they are normally scheduled to add another incentive for tourism, which encourages an artificial staging of local customs. There are renowned fairs in all the regions of Spain. Perhaps the most archetypical is that of Seville, which is also, like the festival of El Rocío, a type of public celebration composed of many private festivities. Only the so-called *real*, or common parade, establishes a certain collective intercommunication. However, the sum total of the individual festivities taking place in private *casetas*, or booths, consolidates and gives substance to the end result. The present-day dance, the echo of the noble *seguidilla* dances from La Mancha, very skillfully popularized by Sevillian girls, the profusion of carriages and riders, and the abundant consumption of wine all combine in a street spectacle, a type of self-complacent theater depicting a society of great hedonism, in which actors and spectators are generally very well delimited.

Maypoles and May Crosses

Spanish collections of traditional songs and ballads abound in references to the month of May and its most famous human correspondences. May encompasses a divergent series of themes, from praise for the gifts of nature to the correlative attributes of love. May, the setting of the florid display of nature and the plenary sign of love, was transformed by the Church into the month of Mary. In May blooms the cult of the protective tree, in modern times reincarnated in the festivity of the May crosses; in May is reborn the ancient beliefs in the plant and water symbols of fertility, transmuted into offerings to the Virgin. The maypole festivities, stemming from that same ritual source, have been celebrated for centuries in all parts of Spain, and their gradual Christianization has only diverted, without altering their basis, their ritualistic path.

Linked by their significance as nature cults to the preceding flower festivals and the gallant placing of garlands, the maypole festivities enjoy an extensive popular appeal. Beginning on the night of April 30, there resound throughout Spain songs — "tomorrow May enters/dressed in flowers" — also called *mayos*, or May songs, wherein nature is praised, the Virgin is exalted, and young girls are serenaded. In La Maragatería, a town in the region of León, and in some towns of Burgos and Palencia, the term *mayo* also signifies the figure, either male or female, placed atop a pole before which dances and merrymaking celebrate the renewed appearance of flowers and fruit. In other Galician localities of Orense and La Coruña, instead of a figure, the *mayo* is a little boy covered with branches and clusters of leaves reverentially cut in the countryside expressly for this purpose. The vegetal disguise here also possesses the force of an allegorical dehumanization of nature.

The principal meaning of *mayo* undoubtedly refers to the tree cut down on the mountain and placed in the main square of the town — a task frequently entrusted to members of the military — coinciding at times with other celebrations not necessarily springlike in essence. Decorated with fruit and garlands, this tree symbolizes a collective hope for fertility. Erected in the most prominent site of many Spanish towns, the tree will remain until the end of May, or even for the entire year, as the vegetal representation of life and, at the same time, as a renewed tribute to the bounteous earth. In front of this tree, a whole series of songs and dances focusing on the rural community's particular anecdotes of each spring are performed.

Love commonly enters the rituals ascribed to these festivals. The wedding of a *mayo* and a *maya* — a young boy and girl of the town — along with the practices of the cult of nature constitute the two main axes on which these centuries-old celebrations turn. The *maya* is the protagonist of a great many of these festivities. Her election, corresponding to the prettiest girl in the town, occasions a series of ceremonies of manifestly pagan origin, already integrated into the Christian practices belonging to this month. While remaining true to the same traditional basis, this celebration, which ranges from the Atlantic coast of Spain to the Mediterranean, has managed to fit into the popular idiosyncrasies of each region. Generally a form of a tacit erotic ceremony prevails in these nuptial rites — feigned marriages — where the *mayas* are awarded to the highest bidder. The fact that she must accompany and dance only with her mate for the duration of the accepted term is a kind of exclusivity clearly connected with some primitive models of sexuality. Gonzalo Correas, in his *Vocabulario de refranes* of the mid-1620s, observed that this purported union of "*mayos* and *mayas* had its beginning in the pagan world, which celebrated Venus in this month."

In some places, mainly in the province of Madrid, not one but several *mayas* are elected. Thrones enveloped in branches and flowers and altars equally covered with lavish decorations are constructed for these girls. The *mayas* appear dressed in the most exquisite costumes of local tradition and bedecked in jewelry. When there are several *mayas*, they must remain motionless in a posture of statuesque dignity, forming something like a multiple allegory of spring, as the *mayeros*, or May participants, dedicate their songs and compliments to them. In the Cuenca region of La Mancha — El Hito, Mota del Cervo — a strange musical instrument called a *tarambel* or *cascabelera*, consisting of a long stick with many cowbells strung on a leather strap, is used as a musical accompaniment for the *mayo* songs. The singular sound of this contraption, a combination of bucolic tones and carnal rings, apparently creates an atmosphere extremely propitious for the passionate intensity of the ceremony.

Some neighborhoods of Madrid practiced an attractive variant of this age-old festival. A group of girls would go to pick up the *maya* at her house, and the boys would carry her on the "queen's little throne" to the site of the celebration, where she would remain, very solemn and still on her seat. In the procession was an old woman bizarrely adorned with strings of garlic, eggshells, and clusters of leaves. Called the *mojigona* (she-devil), she was also enthroned, and must have made a grotesque contrast to the official *maya*, or neighborhood beauty. Today these and other pagan customs, of which there remains but scattered testimony in literature, have already been lost.

Just as the May song is dedicated only to the Virgin, the adoration of the *maya* derived on many occasions from that of the Virgin Mary. A similar transposition occurred with the tree cult, which was transformed into the cult of the holy cross. From this cult sprang the festival of the May cross,

deeply rooted and widespread throughout the different regions of Spain. Connected with the spring festivals of nature, May cross festivities follow a very similar ceremonial pattern and begin on the first of May, the day of Saint James the Less, or on the third, the day of the holy cross, and continue throughout the month of May.

Crosses, as substitutes for the May tree, rise on improvised street altars or in the interior of homes. Each neighborhood or family competes in decorating these altars with all kinds of flowers, trappings, and lights. Different festive practices are carried out around them: dances, banquets, and amatory rituals. In Seville, after a period of decline, May crosses have again appeared with a particular splendor. In some municipalities of Huelva — Alosno, Bonares, Lucena del Puerto — these crosses, set up in a room of the house, are models of craftsmanship and authentic elegance. The culmination of May cross festivities is the "night of favors" on the second Saturday of May. This ceremony, featuring the fandangos typical of the region and bidding for the election of the dancing couple, seems to refer to age-old amatory rituals.

There are also very elaborate May cross festivals in other places in Andalusia, Extremadura, and Murcia. The assimilated elements of Christianized naturist practices are very much in evidence, such as the blessing of the fields and the archaic and widespread rites — so vivid in agrarian cultures — revolving around "May water." Immersing both crosses and images of the Virgin and saints in rivers and fountains is quite traditional in Navarre, the Basque country, Castile, and Extremadura. The pre-Christian vestiges of these rites of prayers for rain are not in doubt. In Caravaca (Murcia), participants plunge a cross into a container full of wine, which becomes transformed into an extremely miraculous beverage. The Vizcayan towns of Lequeitio and Valmaseda utilize the "water of Saint Gregory" — consecrated with the saint's relics — to seek favor for the bounty of the harvests.

A wide range of spring celebrations relate to the

protector saints of agriculture. One of the main exponents could be Saint Isidore, beneficiary of a centuries-old and picturesque devotion in Madrid. During this period other usages and customs clearly connected to cattle-raising also abound, as, for example, the Galician *rapa das bestas* (shearing of the animals). Wild horses are led down from the mountain to the *curros* (corrals), where their manes and tails are cut. It is truly a spectacular operation, combining great dexterity and excitement. Around this celebration has prospered an ersatz pilgrimage or fair. The most notable *curros* are those held on Sundays in May and June in Bayona-Oya, Gondomar, and San Lorenzo de Sabucedo–La Estrada (Pontevedra), Cedeira (La Coruña), and San Andrés de Boimente–Vivero (Lugo). In the Asturian mountain range of Sueves a few remaining herds of wild horses exist — the fabled *asturcones* — already on the path to extinction.

Bulls

With the arrival of fair weather begins what journalists call the bullfighting season. This is not the place to examine in detail this extraordinary and passionate rite, named — rightly or wrongly — the "national fiesta." Clearly, bullfighting entails an authentic mass phenomenon that sparks the most contrary opinions. Despite the strength and depth of its roots in the popular culture, there are those who detest the cruel, bloody nature of the festivity. In any case, bullfighting continues to be one of Spain's greatest festive celebrations, and it is unlikely that any of the periodic antibullfighting campaigns will jeopardize its survival for the foreseeable future.

Independent of the sacred origin of Cretan bullfighting practices and their value as an initiation symbol in many ancient mythologies, both games and confrontations with bulls were very traditional in Spain from the Middle Ages onward. Modern bullfights, however, did not attain their already well-differentiated role as a spectacle until the end of the eighteenth century, when Pepe Hillo published his book *Tauromaquia* and the ritual of the fiesta was established and regulated. From then until now, the artistic rank of the bullfight has been upheld, and its popular echo has only increased, subject to passing periods of splendor and decadence.

One could say much about the significance of bulls, particularly the aesthetic and conceptual guidelines of that contest between man and animal, balanced between "la suerte o la muerte" (*la suerte*, besides referring to the various formal stages of the bullfight, also means luck or fate, the alternative being death). However, let it suffice to repeat that the ritual of bullfighting, which, in its polarities of fear and valor, strength and weakness, art and professionalism produces such a thrill, comes to represent one of the most concealed and symptomatic bases of that chimeric entity that many call the national soul.

Bulls are almost indispensable in any of the major festivals celebrated in the cities and towns of Spain. From the beginning of spring until well into autumn, bullfights assume a festive itinerary of the first magnitude. Naturally, the contests are of varied importance, the most outstanding found in the provincial capitals of Madrid, Seville, Valencia, Bilbao, Barcelona, Saragossa, Málaga, Albacete, Salamanca, Toledo, and Pamplona. Aside from these, one can attend innumerable bullfighting festivities — contests with young bulls, the penning of the bulls, bulls of fire, bulls with their horns covered with wooden balls, bull lassoings, amateur bullfights, and so on — throughout Spain. These will be described in their proper time frame, of summer or fall, but it would be inopportune to sidestep the list of the most attractive festivities — those held in Ciudad Rodrigo (Salamanca), Medinaceli (Soria), Arcos de la Frontera (Cádiz), Cuéllar (Segovia), Brihuega (Guadalajara), Nogueruelas (Teruel), Denia (Alicante), Coria (Cáceres), Fuentesaúco (Zamora), Tordesillas and Peñafiel (Valladolid), and Altura (Castellón).

SUMMER FESTIVALS

The popular festivals of summer grow directly from those of springtime, in general presenting more intense versions of the earlier sun rituals and their various related ceremonies. At the same time, maypole and flower festivals culminate in celebrations of the height of the growing season and the beginning of the harvest, whose rituals of an agrarian nature and of love (courtship and marriage) relate to the earlier festivities. This is also the season when the bonfires peculiar to the summer solstice connect with the world of nature through the "trees of fire" — the *farells*, which means little lighthouses, of numerous Catalonian towns — and many other bonfires of similar meaning. Here again, centuries-old beliefs in the purifying symbols of the flames have been integrated into ecclesiastical rituals. The principal summer festivals adopted by the liturgical calendar are Corpus Christi, Saint John's Day (June 24), the feast day of the Virgin of Mount Carmel (July 16), Saint James's Day (July 25), Saint Ann's Day (July 26), the feast day of the Assumption (August 15), and the numerous variants of patron saints' festivities on September 8.

Before making more generalizations about summer festivals, it is appropriate to add a reminder that the classification of the festive year in seasonal cycles is a convenience and not a rule. Summer, no doubt because of its greater availability of leisure time and its greater ties with nature, is the season best known for its festivals. But spring is also well known. Even winter, between Christmas and Carnival, can assert its claim as bringing together a body of traditional celebrations that can compete in intensity, if not in quantity, with those of spring and summer. It is important to keep in mind that the models and patterns of festivities are extensively interrelated, and that they all arise from the human response to nature's changes and stimuli.

A people, in its highest sense considered as a repository or restorer of a more or less cultural legacy, conceives the festival as an exception to the daily routine. The demands of everyday life are set aside to put into practice simple or complex rituals, be they of religious character or of clearly pagan association. But it is not always the weather that stimulates that unquenchable collective tendency to communicate — consciously or unconsciously — with the supernatural or to choose one amusement or diversion from so many other possibilities. The limits between spring and summer festivals can be very hazy; in fact, until the seventeenth century people called *verano*, or summer, what today is called *primavera*, or spring, and instead of *verano*, they used *estío*, now considered a literary term. Therefore, the clues for holding celebrations as often depend on customs and beliefs based on agricultural practices or rites of a nebulous pagan origin that have been Christianized.

Folklorists, nonetheless, seem to prefer a classification of popular festivals that follows the sun calendar, and it is reasonable to follow their example. In the case of festivals that straddle two seasons, they have been included in the cycle that seems more coherent.

Corpus Christi

The celebration of Corpus Christi — fixed on the Thursday following the week of Pentecost — normally precedes the summer solstice by a few days, but it is already a wholly sun festival in a certain sense: the public adoration of the "body of Christ" triumphantly carried through the streets. Coinciding with the splendor of the cycle of the harvest, whose fruits embellish the holiday in tapestries of wild plants, floral decorations, and street garlands, the festival of the Eucharist is doubtless one of the major milestones of the liturgical year. Although it has recently been eliminated as a holiday from the work calendar, the festivity continues to be celebrated with due pomp and ceremony in the farthest reaches of Christendom. As for Spain, the most renowned celebrations of Corpus Christi may well be those of Toledo, Barcelona, Granada, Saragossa, Seville, and Valencia, not to mention the local variations too numerous to enumerate.

It appears that Barcelona and Gerona were the first two cities to celebrate the public exhibition of the Eucharist with jubilant festivity, which later extended to many other regions. The ceremonies linked to the Thursday of Corpus Christi, or that week, at times denote a type of fusion of religious and profane symbols — that ever so frequent and revealing syncretism — whose practices became interchanged among different localities. Although this feast day was regulated in 1311 by Pope Clement V, and its traditional basis is decidedly Christian, a series of additional aspects deriving from various folkloric sources subsisted. Some of these were, on occasion, prohibited, beginning with the Council of Trent (1545–63), although many others survived, once they were readapted to the Church's liturgical demands or limits of tolerance, if they were not ostensibly changed in meaning.

Documentation exists for many of those ancient practices incorporated into the later Christian commemoration of Corpus Christi, that is, the processional journey of the monstrance through the adorned streets. These festive additions more or less associated with the celebration of Corpus Christi can be summed up as follows: the symbolic representation of animals — tarascas, or dragons, horses, mules, eagles, bulls — the staging of liturgical dramas, mysteries, and other plays with dance; contests of giants and cabezudos, or large-headed dwarfs; processions of mojigones (devils), mojarrillas (jesters), and other burlesque figures; a profusion of floral decorations; and peasant dances then joined with others of a courtly nature. The uncertain origin of all these nonreligious elements became integrated into Corpus Christi with a new symbolism, whether adoration, the triumph of good over evil, or votive offering. The "official" escorts for the procession — members of religious brotherhoods, representatives of town or state gov-

ernment — already come under different protocols.

The most famous tarascas — whose name derives from Tarascon, a city in Provence, France — appear, or used to appear, in the Corpus Christi festivals of Toledo, Madrid, Seville, Barcelona, and San Sebastián, among others. A frightful contraption with the figure of a dragon, probably linked to the magic rites of the solstice, the tarasca was retained in the Corpus Christi celebration as a useful representative of Heresy vanquished by Faith. The same symbolism was preserved in many masks of devils and fantastic animals twisting and turning to escape from the triumphal path of the monstrance, like the monster called Coca, the Galician word for dragon, from Redondela (Pontevedra), a devourer of the imprudent, or Mulasa from Berga (Barcelona), a type of zoological beast that vomits fire. The Colacho from Castrillo (Burgos) is a devil that leaps on children lying on the ground, freeing them from certain ailments. Other mojigones and animal figures from different towns in Valencia, Andalusia, or Extremadura carry scant theological disguise, devoting their energies to scaring spectators. The masks, so generalized not only on Carnival but on many other occasions, reappear here as one furtive festive attraction.

Dances and stagings of plays are intimately linked to Corpus Christi, not so much on account of their religious nature as for their association with the summer festival. In these stagings — liturgical dramas, mysteries — Eucharistic themes or themes of Biblical history predominate, and in the dances one customarily gleans an additional meaning: the struggle between the angel and the devil, salvation and hell, grace and sin. Certain ancient warlike recollections come through in many of these dances, others were proscribed by some intolerant bishop. Among the many examples are the Corporales of Daroca (Saragossa), the Dance of the Sixes from Seville, the Turcs i Caballets, or Turks and Little Horses, of Berga (Barcelona), the Sant Joan Palos i les Aguiles (Saint John Palos and the Eagles) from Pollensa (Mallorca), the Paloteos (Wrangling) from

Fuentepelayo (Segovia), the Pecados y Virtudes (Sins and Virtues) from Camuñas (Toledo), the *dantzaris* (dancers) from Oñate (Guipúzcoa), the Ball de Bastons (Dance of the Sticks) of Solsona (Lérida), and the Danza de la Cruz (Dance of the Cross) of Valverde de los Arrollos (Badajoz).

San Juan (Saint John's Day)

The celebration of the summer solstice is almost universal. Ancient rites linked to the mythic triumph of light over the shadows were recast and popularized in Christianity by means of the festivity of Saint John's Day, coinciding with the shortest night of the year. Between June 23 and 24, fire illuminates a good part of Spain. Perhaps only in Andalusia, whose people, unlike the Arabs of earlier times, are not fond of playing with fire, is this omnipresent ritual downplayed. While bonfires form part of many other festivals, those of Saint John's Day carry the most traditional significance in the folkloric customs of the solstice.

Fire alone, however, does not take center stage, for water and sun also have cults identified basically with the practices of Saint John's Day. The night-time ceremonies of the bonfires are frequently accompanied by rites to the sun and to water. The custom of gathering beside the sea, or by a river or fountain, to see the sun set apparently derives from centuries-old pre-Christian cults. These ancestral traditions of Saint John's Day, profusely collected in the literature of medieval and Renaissance Spain, continue to possess a certain magical character, in very different types of ceremonies: curative, prophetic, and initiatory. The belief that on that day the sun dances on the horizon is still widespread in rural areas, for example, in Caravia (Asturias), Alquia (Guipúzcoa), San Juan (Mallorca), with its very strange Festa d'es Sol Qui Balla (Festival of the Dancing Sun), Herrera del Duque (Badajoz), Alegría de Alava, and many other Galician towns. Besides this cult to the sun linked to fire, a parallel

and very primitive one is dedicated to water or fountains. (All this has been studied with superb insight by the eminent critic Julio Caro Baroja in his work titled *La estación de amor*, or The Season of Love.)

From the *nit del foc* (night of fire) of different towns in Barcelona, Valencia, and Alicante — so fond of real fires as well as fireworks — to the *cachelas* of Carballo (La Coruña); from the *fuegos del santo* (saint's fires) of Eibar (Guipúzcoa) to the *fallas* (bonfires) of the Pyrenees near Lérida; from the *lucernas* (lanterns) of Poyo (Pontevedra) to the *calderas* (cauldrons) of Soria; from the *bolas de fuego* (fireballs) of Icod de los Vinos (Tenerife) to the *achiperres* of Salamanca, the fires of the solstice constitute one of the oldest and most varied folkloric manifestations in Spain's calendar of festivals.

Another ancient tradition stemming from the summer solstice, "recreated" by the Church within the festivals dedicated to Saint John, consists of excursions into the countryside to look for medicinal flowers and herbs. Examples from popular collections of songs and ballads referring to some lyrical or amatory episode occurring on Saint John's night or morning are legion, some readjusted within that interpretative duality of the month of flowers/month of Mary. The cult of herbs, linked to medical or prophetic rites — elixirs of love, practices of folk medicine, spells — goes back centuries. Verbena, basil, clover, elder, valerian, rosemary, and lemon verbena play an important magical-symbolic role in many celebrations of summer.

Among the festivals of Saint John, that complex union of dissimilar elements, those of San Pedro Manrique (Soria) and Ciudadela (Menorca), although very influenced by touristic demands, preserve solid roots in centuries-old local traditions. In San Pedro Manrique, once the bonfire is consumed, a tapestry of ashes is formed on which the youths of the town, sometimes barefoot, other times carrying another person astride, will walk. It is said that only the *pasadores* (those who walk over the ashes) of San Pedro emerge unscathed from such a fearless purification test. This celebration culminates the next morning with another ritual of a very different nature: that of the *móndidas* (a virgin offered to Arab chiefs), in which three girls, dressed in white and wearing a large floral basket crowned with loaves of bread, recite and dance to commemorate the cancellation of a legendary medieval tribute known as the "hundred damsels." The Saint John's festival in Ciudadela is very different but equally spectacular. It centers on an impressive street exhibition whose main character is the horse. Its ceremony is very strict and dramatically highlights the hierarchical differences of Ciudadela society. In these equestrian games, which display a pronounced medieval flavor, the *cavallers*, or knights, and the different *caixers*, or masters of ceremonies, partake in a type of tournament of skill and daring, whose principal feats are the *ensortillá*, or threading a ring with a lance, the *abraçats*, or the galloping of two embraced riders, and the *caragols*, or the beautiful but threatening prancing of the horses amid the impassioned spectators.

Apart from all this, common events in the various versions of these festivals, for example, as the entrance or epilogue for the crucial moment when the bonfires burn, include dances, the placing of garlands, the blessing of the fields, curative and amatory rites, roped bulls, the burning of figures, the expectance of apparitions, and flagellation for the expulsion of evil spirits. From this one can deduce that the multiform character of the Saint John's festival is like a summary of the principal customs and beliefs that became fused in the festivals of the summer solstice.

Calendar of Saints' Days of Summer Festivals

Many Spanish towns celebrate their patron saints' festivities in the summer. Here follows just a few of them, perhaps not the most famous but at least the most characteristic. On June 29, the feast day of Saint Peter, patron of fishermen,

there proliferate some curious coastal festivities, in certain towns shifted to July 16, the feast day of the Virgen del Carmen (Virgin of Mount Carmel), also patron saint of this profession. Excursions on garland-laden boats, processions, and rites of blessing the sea are the principal events of the commemoration. In Catalonia, notably the Festas dels Pescadors (Festivities of the Fishermen) are quite traditional, as are those in the Basque country. For example, in Lequeitio (Vizcaya), the appointment of the stewards of the ancient Brotherhood of Seafarers is evoked with the dance of the *kaxarranca*, executed on a large chest carried by eight fishermen on their shoulders.

Coinciding with the feast day of Saint Peter, people in Haro (La Rioja) celebrate a traditional *batalla del vino* (battle of the wine). As the name indicates, the superb Rioja wine is not only drunk but is spilled in strange "watering" contests between the participating formations. Around this time, the *amuravela* (tacking the sail), whose maritime atmosphere is fused with a type of satiric chronicle of the year's local events, takes place in Cudillero (Asturias). In the town of Grao (Castellón), the seaside procession of Saint Peter is accompanied by a "bull of fire," which the most daring participants whip with a furious violence proper to the occasion. Days later, other bulls (those of Saint Fermin) will run.

Although the running of the bulls takes place in numerous municipalities of the Basque country and Navarre — Lesaca, Pasajes de San Pedro — that of the city of Pamplona, known as *sanfermines*, or Saint Fermin's, is, by definition, the quintessential example. Saint Fermin is a very authentic Pamplona saint. Serving as the town's first bishop, he evangelized the area, the Roman Pampelo, with extreme zeal and suffered martyrdom without the slightest fear, making him a model well suited to an enterprise calling up proofs of intrepidity. From the starting signal of the *chupinazo* (loud bang) on July 6, the entire city becomes a swarm of youth, either in groups from clubs or alone. Each morning a herd of bulls, escorted by the *cabestros*, or leaders, appears. The ensuing supreme display of Pamplona bravery tests each youth's skill at teasing the bulls yet avoiding their horns as he runs in front of them. Afterward, all dissolves in an endless celebration for the participants of these clubs, as they sing and dance constantly and undergo a type of contest to outdo each other at drinking and eating.

This ritual of man facing the bull probably dates back centuries and no doubt derives from ancestral practices, but the sociological flux and flow of the Pamplona runnings certainly endow the festival with a very complex ingredient of exhibitionism. Especially beginning with the propaganda disseminated by Ernest Hemingway, the *sanfermines* festival was transformed into a vaguely bookish tourist attraction that placed a mistaken emphasis on the exhibition of an entire population's "manliness." Those foreigners who wander around the packed streets of Pamplona in an advanced state of inebriation play the role of impromptu extras in a secular tradition determined by one or another hybrid social stimulus.

On July 22, the feast day of the Magdalene, a truly attractive series of ceremonies unfolds in Anguiano (La Rioja). A group of dancers, wearing skirts and standing on stilts, dance before the saint and undertake a hazardous and dizzying race around the slopes and stairs surrounding the church. It is really a ritual in which skill is fused with ancient votive practices that somehow recall the frenzied whirling of the dervishes.

The night of Saint James and Saint Ann — July 25 and 26 — holds a certain magical connotation in some towns, especially if it coincides with a full moon, that mythical dispenser of good luck and misfortune. While the city of Santiago de Compostela accords it a solemn commemoration, a more flamboyant group of festivals programmed for these days, or the last two weeks of July, can be easily enumerated, ranging from the night-long *flamenco*, or gypsy, celebration of Saint Ann in the Seville neighborhood of Triana to the ferocious

decapitation of geese from horseback in El Carpio de Tajo (Toledo); from the pilgrimage for rain in San Benito de Lérez (Pontevedra) to the previously mentioned processions by the sea in honor of the Virgen del Carmen; from the "descent of the branch" in Agaete (Gran Canaria), with all its pre-Hispanic cults of supplication for rain, to the Catalonian Festa dels Raiers, or Festival of the Raftsmen, in Pobla de Segur (Lérida), in which the raftsmen evoke the transportation of tree trunks on the Noguera Pallaresa River. And this does not include the festival of August 15 — Festival of the Virgin of the Assumption, or the Virgin of August — when innumerable Spanish cities and towns celebrate their saints' day festivities. Among the theatrical stagings associated with this day, the *loa* (playlet) of La Alberca (Salamanca) and the *misteri* (mystery play in Valencian) of Elche (Alicante) still display popular vestiges of medieval theater.

FALL FESTIVALS

Not surprisingly, festivals decline in the fall. As the warm caresses of summer recede and the first twinges of cold weather appear, occasions of collective diversion seem to diminish. One could almost venture the assertion that as summer, that period of programmed leisure and the distractions of vacation, draws to a close, life reverts to its daily routine and the tendency for public merriment effectively declines. Not that festivals from the religious and lay calendar of Spain disappear; rather, the occasions, and also, in a certain sense, the stimuli simply grow scarcer. Something akin to the fatigue after a period of merriment filters through the subconscious of a people.

Except for some regions in the south, the earth has fully yielded its fruits. Until the time for new sowing and related farm chores, nature, like people, asks for a rest. One has the impression that there is little to celebrate until the Christmas season approaches. Only the earlier agrarian celebrations linked to the diverse summer harvests are perhaps briefly continued in similar festivities, for example, in some late harvests or in the *monda de la rosa de azafrán* (pruning of the saffron rose), commemorated in Consuegra (Toledo) on the last Sunday of October.

Very probably the lack, or paucity, of collective festivals in autumn is a stimulus for games of a private or individual nature, that is, pastimes spent in the more or less relative intimacy of the casino, the café, or the family gathering. It is well known that the tendency to choose a particular game serves, in a certain way, as a barometer to define the innate behavior, reactions, and life-styles of a community. For example, the fact that in the Basque country people enjoy sports or amusements related to physical stamina — cutting tree trunks, lifting weights, pulling boulders — is an integral part of their character. Another example in a similar vein is the affinity of Spain's Mediterranean towns for fireworks. A festivity there without the greatest possible number of fireworks explosions is simply inconceivable. On the last night of Saint John's, six million fireworks were detonated in Catalonia, which makes one think of an all-too-frequent disposition for using noise as the principal vehicle for communication.

Although private amusements are most abundant between the autumn equinox and the summer solstice, it is still not difficult to highlight some memorable celebrations, both religious and lay, during these months. From the point of view of frequency, these months could very well be called transitional, a transition in which towns anticipate or extend commemorations related to other seasonal cycles: masquerades, fairs, pilgrimages, the running of bulls, and bonfires. While they may not be numerous, fall festivals include many offering especially significant traits and peculiarities.

In Rus (Jaén) at the very end of September, the Domingo de Mozos (Youth Sunday), a type of strange carnival, is celebrated, while in Petrel (Alicante) *carases*, or masquerade, an antique and strange vestige of carnival, is held beginning on October 7, the day of the Virgin of Victory (now called the Virgin of the Rosary). An example of a spontaneous festival is the Corpus Christi festivity held the last Sunday in October in Fuentelespino de Haro (Cuenca). Nor is there a lack of fairs, especially around Saint Michael's Day (September 29), among which those in Olot (Gerona), Guernica (Vizcaya), and Mondoñedo (Lugo) are significant because of their agrarian or cattle-raising importance.

Apart from the previously mentioned pilgrimage in San Andrés de Teixidó (La Coruña), the procession held on October 5 in Moclín (Granada) is the most curious. An enormous painting of Christ bearing the cross is taken out of the church and on a procession. Even though it was prohibited on more than one occasion, the citizens of Moclín, however, never gave up this strange pilgrimage of somewhat fetishistic aspect, for they attribute to the devout cult of this image all types of sudden cures of female sterility, the treatments including varied clandestine amatory practices. This seems to be a genuine case of an ancient medical-carnal ritual that has been ingeniously Christianized.

In some towns in the province of Toledo, on the night of November 1 and 2 — the Day of the Dead — inhabitants set out to fill in keyholes with *puches*, or a floury dough, to keep the very tenuous souls in purgatory from entering. The stories of these souls are recounted around the fireplace, where chestnuts are roasted. People in these parts cite the proverb, "El día de los finados, andan los muertos por los tejados" (On the Day of the Dead, the dead roam over the roofs). To counteract the effects of these spirits, large and small bells are rung, and butterflies are set on fire in pots of oil placed at the door of the house, as youths disguised as phantoms set out to scare their neighbors. Days later, when these souls in purgatory have returned to their resting places, the *auroros* (dawn signers) come out before daybreak to sing to the Virgin and, incidentally, to the village girls, especially in different towns in La Mancha. In Lorca (Murcia), the bands of *auroros* would go through the streets singing their *trovos* (poems) on Saturdays between the Immaculate Conception (December 8) and Candlemas Day (February 2). They carried lanterns and were accompanied by a strange instrument, the *zaramangüel*, or small guitar, which has since practically disappeared.

On October 12, the feast day of the Virgen del Pilar (Virgin of the Pillar), and apart from the official festivities scheduled in Saragossa — "the glass rosary," dances, and offerings of flowers — inhabitants sing, pray, and hold outdoor celebrations in other towns of Spain. The feast day of the Virgin of the Pillar is not, however, a festivity of traditionally popular roots. The fact that the Franco government bureau of festivals had it coincide with the event of such patriotic nature as the Day of the Race or Day of the Hispanic World no doubt helped to lend a rhetorical note of governmental authority to the celebration.

Few other festivals fit in the time frame of autumn. But there are some runnings of bulls of extreme interest that depart from their habitual spring or summer cycle, for example the *toro embolado* (bull with wooden balls on his horns) in Mora de Rubielos (Teruel), the *encierro de vaquillas* (running of the heifers) in Alcaudete de la Jara (Toledo), and particularly the aforementioned and fascinating *toro júbilo* (bull with balls of burning pitch and resin on its horns) in Medinaceli (Soria), held on the Saturday before November 13. Perhaps the last relevant festival in autumn is the Immaculate Conception. In the town of Horcajo de Santiago (Cuenca), it is celebrated in a very personal and emblematic way — with the *vítor*, a series of stentorian shouts of joy to the Virgin of the Immaculate Conception inside the church, after which the town's youths engage in a fierce struggle to keep the processional banner from being taken out into the street. When this finally happens, the banner is taken by "three knights," who, after being feted, ride through the town all night long.

Other festive contributions to the religious ceremony of the Immaculate Conception include the *encamisás* (disguises) in Torrejoncillo and Holguera (Cáceres), the offerings of pastry rings and fruit in Aldeanueva de Atienza (Guadalajara), the bonfires of Miguelturra (Ciudad Real), and the *misa de pajes* (pages' mass) in Yecla (Murcia). And already, while the slaughtering of animals is being celebrated, with its additional repertory of rituals linked to some mortal sin or other, we arrive at winter.

After the autumn period, which, save for isolated instances, holds little of particular relevance from the point of view of festivals, comes another of the great moments of the Western liturgical calendar: the period between Christmas and Carnival. Both celebrations, of the jubilant birth of Christ and the exaltation of liberty prior to the restrictions of Lent, are no doubt the two principal winter festivities, if not the most widely celebrated in all of Christendom.

A counterpart to the tendency toward fewer celebrations in the transition from summer to autumn is a reawakened predisposition for the festival as inclement weather intensifies. It is as though the celebrants had rested sufficiently, and, once the relative calm of autumn was superseded, the excuses (justified or not) for collective merriment were reborn. Until the Lenten edicts of abstinence and seclusion officially begin, all presumed leisure moments are translated into an almost endless occasion for celebrating something: Christmas, the vestiges of the Saturnalia in the Day of the Innocents (December 28), a new year, Epiphany, some saint's day or other, and finally, the lengthy counterweights of Lent...Thus, this festive current of winter is enlarged, fragmented in numerous celebrations: offerings, *obispillos* (youths playing the role of the bishop), varied games of masquerades, *fiestas de locos* (festivities of the mad), bonfires, versions of popular theater, holy bread, carnival, symbolic cults to animals.

Winter is, to a certain contradictory extent, a festive time: cold weather and snow seem to counsel going out as little as possible, but the popular spirit incites the opposite. In the Festival of the First Flower (the almond), celebrated in some towns of Valencia on February 2 (Candlemas Day), the ostensible reason for the outing seems somewhat exaggerated. However, this "first flower" undoubtedly symbolizes a festive desire discovering one of its most notable paths of winter merriment.

Christmas is one of the basic milestones of the festive cycles referred to. It seems that such a symbolic anniversary was established precisely on the days bordering the winter solstice in order to neutralize the importance of an ancient sun cult celebrated during the same period in the pagan world. In any case, this festivity, once Christianized, was imported into Spain at the end of the fourth century and has survived undiminished.

Along general lines, the Christmas period contains a body of celebrations held from the evening of December 24 — that is, coinciding with the winter solstice — until January 6, the feast day of the Three Magi. There is no town in Spain, or any other Western country, that does not commemorate the birth of Christ in some fashion, be it in its theological aspect or through highly diluted profane diversions. Its overriding importance is the manifestation of a shared jubilation that already, here and there, has modified its original reason for being, becoming confused with that other reverential cult to the continuity of life symbolized by the new year.

Within the natural similarity of background of the different Christmas celebrations, there exist many variants of a popular character. The obviously fixed elements pose no obstacle to the development of other modes of merriment exclusive to specific regions. The *villancico*, or Christmas carol, one of Spain's most eminent sources of popular poetry, resounds on these days from one extreme of the country to the other, in the different versions appertaining to their respective musical collections of poetry. In the lands of Andalusia, Extremadura, and Murcia — that is, in regions of more benign climate — groups of revelers go out into the streets with musical selections and requests for gifts. Nowadays very rare, *zambombas*, or rustic drum parties, took place in different Sevillian neighborhood patios, not only on Christmas Eve or New Year's Eve but on many other days during the Christmas cycle, offering participants the opportunity to dance, sing, and drink. With a meaningful frequency, the festivities were entrusted to the gypsies, whose peculiar and jocular manner of commemorating Christmas constitutes a particularly important, centuries-old religious assimilation.

The *misa del gallo*, or Midnight mass — literally, mass of the rooster; the first cry of the cock, according to tradition, is heard at midnight — or the masses of joys (of the Virgin Mary) from the region of La Mancha generally precede the public or private festivities of Christmas Eve. In many places, the celebration goes out into the street, with performances, scheduled or improvised, of dances and songs by groups of bell ringers, pastoral plays, groups of merrymakers, bands of strolling musicians, and dawn bells. Theatrical performances also abound, especially in Catalonia, where scenes on the theme of Christmas are acted out, such as the *pessebres* (manger scenes in Catalonian) or *pastorets* (pastoral playlets). Numerous towns in the provinces of Toledo and Guadalajara have their *nacimientos vivientes*, or live nativity scenes, or liturgical Christmas plays, in Galisteo (Cáceres) or Marjaliza (Toledo). A ritual of special interest, held in parts of Navarre and Guipúzcoa, features the *olentzaro*, or coal miner, who comes down the mountain to the town to announce the joyful tidings of the birth of Christ.

Palma de Mallorca's *cant de la Sibil·la* (song of the sybil), just one among the innumerable different celebrations that lead up to Christmas, is an ancient prophetic rite prohibited in its time by the Council of Trent. However, thanks to an easygoing bishop, it took root in Mallorca, where it is still performed in the cathedral. An altar boy, elegantly dressed, sings an ancient melody, part prophetic, part apocalyptic, from the pulpit.

December 28, the Day of the Innocents, brings forth traditional jokes and deceits, from the most innocuous to the most virulent. A sampling includes *fiestas de locos* (festivities of the mad), *obispillos* (boys playing the role of the bishop), masquerades, election of the monarchs, mayors, and other burlesque figures, giving something of a foretaste of Carnival, which, according to Julio Caro Baroja, is linked to the Roman Saturnalia. The festivities of the mad are, of course, extremely remote in origin and still survive, for better or worse, in some towns of Spain; those held in Ecija (Seville) or Campo de Mirra (Alicante) are perhaps the most spectacular. In Alicante province, lively masquerades are also organized: the *enfarinats* (in Valencian, those covered with flour) hand out fines and read their mordant edicts, while the *tapats* (the disguised) create havoc on the streets. In Yeste (Albacete) the *calentureros* (goaders), masked figures with whips, pursue those who resist paying a contribution.

The festivities of the *obispillos* have practically died out, but some vestiges survive, like the Bisbetó (Little Bishop in Catalonian) of Montserrat. From time immemorial, they used to be celebrated inside or around the cathedral and featured a boy invested with a certain feigned authority who delivered a series of pointed jokes and generally made mischief. Seville became notorious for these festivities, which were banned by the Church at the end of the seventeenth century. Similar in character is the election of the monarchs — for example the *faba* (bean king) in Navarre, the *porqueros* (pigmen's king) in Madrid, and the *mazarrón* (toll or tax cheat) in Burgos — although the main actor is no longer a boy, and many other more shameless burlesque displays of authority are permitted.

New Year's Eve, as the departure of one year and the welcoming of another, carries a special meaning and follows a wide variety of rituals. In a certain way, this is a celebration of markedly conventional nature, although there persist abundant practices of clearly symbolic origin, all linked to the cyclical renewal of life. For example, besides the worldly festivities, many towns have practices related to the spring, referring basically to fire and the tree. Hence, there are pine festivities in Cogollos de Guadix (Granada) called La Carretá (Cart Load); several ancient dances of pastoral flavor offered to the Christ child on December 25 in Isso (Albacete); a procession of youths carrying a pine tree down from the mountain to the noisy accompaniment of *trabucaires* (blunderbuss carriers) in Centelles (Barcelona); or the burning of the *castillos del santo* (saint's castle) with pine branches in Huesa (Jaén). Perhaps this centuries-old habit of decorating trees and lighting bonfires in times of cold weather or drought arises from the converse symbolic commemoration of the annual "renewal" of life.

With the first days of the new year, the *botargas*, or devils, return to the lands of Castile and La Mancha. Perhaps the most characteristic example is that of Veldenuño Fernández (Guadalajara), where a female devil, carrying a club, castanets, and cowbells, performs a series of leaps in front of the church congregation and feigns a ferocious battle with a group of dancers representing Virtue. Likewise, several venerable dances called expressly Dances of the (Christ) Child are performed in some towns in the province of Albacete, including Isso and Caudete.

On January 6, the day of the Epiphany, the famed tradition of the liturgical dramas of the Three Magi is repeated in different towns. These dramas are still performed with a varying degree of fidelity in Santillana del Mar (Cantabria), Sangüesa (Navarre), Vianos (Albacete), Cañada (Alicante), Churra (Murcia), and Viso de los Pedroches (Córdoba). The proverbial cavalcades have acquired more modern, official practices, their rituals depending on the tastes and habits of each region. Currently, some of them are also celebrated in rural areas, the corteges and Oriental costumes arousing excitement in the children.

Moros y Cristianos (Moors and Christians)

Coinciding with the Day of the Three Magi, the initial cycle of the Moors and Christians festivities begins in Cuenca, specifically in Valverde de Júcar. Because it is a very significant early celebra-tion leading to many others of the same type, disseminated profusely through different regions of Spain, it is included in the winter cycle although it is celebrated practically all year long.

The Moors and Christians festivals, evocative of very old border confrontations during the period of Islamic domination in the Iberian Peninsula, have their purported origin in the reed games that began to proliferate in the sixteenth century. These games consisted of a feigned battle between two forces that used reeds instead of lances. The knights of one of the forces dressed in Moorish garb, and the others were attired in Castilian (i.e., Christian) vestments.

The festival of this type par excellence is that held in Alcoy (Alicante). The extravagance of the disguises of the different battling troops, the more or less carnivalesque street atmosphere, and the costly consumption of gunpowder lend this celebration a patently baroque, Mediterranean character. Other towns along the Mediterranean also feature their corresponding local copies of Moors and Christians, as can be seen in the different towns of the provinces of Cáceres, Cádiz, Cuenca, Huesca, Almería, Mallorca, Granada, Toledo, Ciudad Real, Teruel, Jaén, Castellón, Valencia, Saragossa, and Orense. In some regions, especially the Alpujarras, in the southern part of the province of Granada, the Moors and Christians festivities habitually consist of a performance of scenes full of local allusions.

Winter Calendar of Saints' Days

The days after the Christmas festivities and before the arrival of Carnival — if they have not already been held, in a reverse chronological order — are filled with celebrations in which practices and customs already mentioned are repeated: *botargas*, or devils, *soldadescas*, or military episodes, Moors and Christians, bonfires, pilgrimages...All coincide with some religious festivity, whose principal markers are the following feast days: Saint Anthony (January 17), Saint Sebastian (January 20), Saint Paul (January 25), Candlemas (February 2), Saint Blas (February 3), and Saint Agatha (February 5).

Around Saint Anthony's Day, the day of Saint Anthony the Abbot, patron of domestic animals, blessings of these animals and the reappearance of ancient ceremonies of bonfires and disguises are very frequent. The blessing of the animals, normally decked out according to local custom, derives obviously from ancient cattle-raising rites and is still very much alive in many regions. The fire cult also incorporated into this festivity doubtless derives from certain purification rites. Indeed, bonfires occupy an important place on Saint Anthony's night. In Alpera (Albacete), an edict proclaimed the night before the festival can serve to gauge its importance: "Whoever goes into the street after 8 P.M. runs the risk of being burned."

Hence, there are many showy bonfires and masquerades around Saint Anthony's Day. In Villanueva de Alcolea (Castellón) or Navalvillar de Pela (Badajoz), horse riders join the game of leaping or avoiding the flames. Days later, in Sigüenza (Guadalajara), revelers light a huge bonfire in front of the so-called Casa del Doncel (House of the Donzel, or young prince) to honor Saint Vincent, the patron of the city. Mallorca enjoys *foguerons* (large bonfires) and *dimonis* (devil) disguises around Saint Anthony's Day, and in Arquillos (Jaén), for the lack of a bonfire, the *pelotero* (ball player), a type of devil who pursues the imprudent, stirs about the streets. The *santantoná*, or Saint Anthony's festival, of some towns in the Maestrazgo area — Mirambel, Forcall, La Mata, Todolella, Villafranca — consists of the performance of scenes from the saint's life and the burning of a large *barraca* (a Valencian house with a steep, pointed roof) built of pine branches. Among the processions of Saint Anthony's, the most dramatic are those in Trigueros (Huelva), where spectators throw money, delectable loaves of bread, fruit, and even hams in

the saint's path; in Balsa de Ves (Albacete), with its rows of children carrying small baskets of blessed bread; or in Mas de las Matas (Teruel), where they escort a *mojiganga*, or mummer, who recites in a provocative manner incidents of local life.

Around Saint Sebastian's and Saint Paul's days, bonfires, masquerades, *botargas* (devils), young bulls, and military episodes again return. The masquerade called *perros e hilanderas* (dogs and spinners) in Santa Ana de Pusa (Toledo) and the *carantoñas* (grotesque masks) from Acehúche (Cáceres) are notable examples, among others, of some old, emblematic ritual: the disguise with animal skins, he-goats, bears, cows, perhaps to assume a more effective identification with the powers of nature. Saint Sebastian — the soldier saint — does not fail to give rise to some procession or another with a certain military air. Among their more interesting manifestations are the renowned *tamborrada* (drumroll) in San Sebastián and showy displays of *botargas* with whips, like the *morraches* in Malpica de Tajo (Toledo), the *jarramplas* in Piornal and Navaconsejo (Cáceres), and the *botarga la larga*, *la Cascarulera* (the tall she-devil, the crusher) in Montarrón (Guadalajara). El Toboso in La Mancha — supposedly the village of Don Quixote's lady, Dulcinea — organizes one of the most eagerly anticipated Spanish carnivals on this day.

In San Pablo de Montes (Toledo), the inhabitants honor their patron, Saint Paul, with a curious festivity called *la vaca* (the cow), a type of masquerade of young men back from their military service. One of these, disguised as a cow, charges out-of-towners who have come to witness the celebration, while another, dressed as a mother pig, devotes himself to lifting women's skirts, part-erotic, part-violent elements that appear in many popular celebrations. In Guarrate (Zamora), the recruits, attired in military garb, run roosters on the last Sunday in January and try to decapitate the birds with a slash from their sabers. The spectacle has its interest from the point of view of local customs, but it is not instructive. The following day in Ituren Zubieta

(Navarre) is the showy festival of the *yoariak* or *zan-panzarrak* (Saint Fatbelly in Basque). These individuals, dressed in petticoats and sheepskins, visit each other in a display of good neighborliness, ringing the enormous cowbells hanging from their backs.

February 2, day of the Purification of the Virgin Mary — Candlemas — witnesses offerings of pigeons and turtledoves, hymns to the Virgin of "Las Purificas," the offering of candied pine-nut rings, miraculous candles to frighten off evils and torments, bonfires, and, of course, *botargas*, persecuting devils. A Castilian legend relates the origin of the *botargas* to the ritual of the Purification of the Virgin Mary: Mary was ashamed to go alone to the temple for the act of purification, once the forty days after childbirth passed, so she had herself accompanied by a grotesque character who would divert people's attention. These *botargas* participate in this festivity in many towns of La Alcarria, the northwestern part of Cuenca province, including Beleña de Sorbe, Arbancón, and Retiendas.

Menasalbas (Toledo) holds a nighttime procession called the *encamisada* (disguised), formed by a cortege of men on horseback who ride through the town illuminated by torches and the light of the bonfires. The *endiablada* (bewitched) procession in Almonacid del Marquesado (Cuenca) features devils that maneuver crazily before the float of the Virgin, making their cowbells ring wildly.

As the protector against illnesses of the throat, Saint Blas is a beloved saint. Legend has it that when he was being led to his martyrdom he saved a child who was choking on a bone. Since then — the beginning of the fourth century — popular imagination has attributed many miraculous cures to this saint. Processions, medical rituals, pilgrimages, and the preparation and blessing of rings and ribbons coincide on this day with new *endiabladas* and performances by dancers. In Porriño (Pontevedra), Peralta and Lodosa (Navarre), Moral de Calatrava (Ciudad Real), Miraflores de la Sierra (Madrid), Ciudad Rodrigo (Salamanca), and Villar del Arzobispo (Valencia), people go out into the countryside on Saint Blas's Day and also hold banquets and blessings of bread and cakes. On Saint Blas's Day — or the next day (sometimes called *resamblás*) — are also performed age-old dances with allusive themes, like those of *los negritos* (little blacks) in Montehermoso (Cáceres) or in Idiazábal (Guipúzcoa).

Women are the main players in the festivity of Saint Agatha, the patron of married women and zealous protector of mothers' breasts. In parts of Segovia, Salamanca, and Zamora, this devotion attains its greatest popularity, although it is also deeply rooted in other towns, like Yélamos de Arriba (Guadalajara) and Alcañiz (Teruel), where they even prepare loaves of bread actually called *tetas de Santa Agueda* (Saint Agatha's teats). In Espinosa de Henares, another town in the region of La Alcarria, women light a great bonfire that the men attempt to put out. Perhaps the most popular of all these festivities is that of Zamarramala (Segovia). Two older, respectable married women lead the ritual of their ephemeral power, attired in splendid local costumes. After a reading of a type of list of complaints against male authority, a stuffed figure is burned.

Carnival

In theory, and according to the liturgical calendar, Carnival embraces the three days preceding Ash Wednesday, the date on which Lent begins. But in practice, Carnival can be celebrated — and indeed is celebrated — when tradition or the whim of each town decides. There are already Carnivals from the beginning of the Christmas cycle, and some even slip right into Lent. Many of the practices previously enumerated — devils, masquerades, festivities of the mad, little bishops — more or less take part in what is commonly identified with the Carnival spirit. However, Carnival has something that differentiates it from other diversions of similar characteristics and lends it an unmistakable psychological aura.

Carnival's universal appeal and its roots in the most varied cultures undoubtedly are based in its transgression of the norm, the subversion of established order. While Carnival in the Christian world held the value of a period of liberty before Lent prohibitions, its ultimate justification is much more complex. Apart from the allegorical combat between Don Carnal (Carnival) and Doña Cuaresma (Lent) that Juan Ruiz, the archpriest of Hita, bequeathed us in his semiautobiographical poem *Libro de buen amor* of the fourteenth century, Carnivals engage other paths of conduct, other emotional stimuli. Its original religious character has remained greatly diluted in this full intensification of the sensual pleasures linked to its pagan roots.

In Carnival almost everything is permitted: its one exception is also rooted in its permissiveness. Before putting on a mask it is imperative to disguise oneself, that is, camouflage one's natural state and aspect. The game consists of altering one's personality, liberating inhibitions, supplanting the "other," even changing sex. The individual who disguises himself becomes that "other" whom he has dared not be in normal circumstances. Hence, the therapeutic meaning of Carnival, its cathartic condition, derives from that alteration, that change of identity.

Much has been said about the origins of, even the etymological base of the word *carnival*. There are those who believe its name derives from the Italian *carne vale* (meat farewell) or from the Latin *carrus navalis*, that is, from the boat raised up on a cart in which Dionysus, or Bacchus, appeared during the festivities in his honor. Julio Caro Baroja, whose studies on Carnival are unsurpassed, affirms that, as we understand it today, Carnival is "a son, even though he is a prodigal son, of Christianity." In any case, that affiliation is not contradicted by the religious alteration of a ritual of manifest pagan roots.

The Spaniard likes to disguise himself for very varied reasons; he does so even when the occasion is not justified. The Arabs were very fond of these sensual and liberating games. What is certain is that from Christmas to Lent, all of peninsular and insular Spain celebrates Carnival with greatly varied forms of merriment. After the severe prohibitions and repression of the Franco years, from 1936 to 1975, these diversions have reemerged as what they always have been: a healthful and playful exaltation essentially integrated into the popular sensibility.

In Galicia, Carnival — known as the Antruejo — is traditionally limited, with rare obedience, to the chronology dictated by the liturgical calendar. In the Basque country and the region of Castile–La Mancha as well, the variable dates preceding Ash Wednesday are respected punctiliously. But in practice, these time limits are exceeded with little objection. Each city, each town celebrates the festivity in its own fashion, with the variations peculiar to its case. Aside from the universally required use of disguises, everything else depends on local idiosyncrasy and capacity for jokes and disrespect. Anything can happen, and the limit of personal freedom is ruled only — and not always — by collective argument. Apart from some specific rituals, with figures and characters linked to the town's tradition, Carnival programs are very varied and might include street bands and masquerades or spectacular processions of carriages and figures; the singing of impudent songs; the flinging of flour, ashes, water, or wine; the tossing of figures in a blanket into the air; feasts; the burning of rag dolls; the running of cocks; dances; and lastly, jests and roguish deeds of a varying nature.

The most renowned Spanish Carnivals are those of Santa Cruz de Tenerife and Cádiz, although perhaps they are not the most clearly linked to age-old popular rites. The Santa Cruz de Tenerife Carnival is one that takes on an aspect of the almost tropical nature of the island and coincides in many aspects with the splendor of Carnival in Rio de Janeiro. The Cádiz Carnival is very different, with its masquerades, choruses, and joking; the whole city becomes a fascinating stage for the exhibition of much wit, jokes, and impudence, which the inhabitants have succeeded in storing up all year long. As is traditional, these Carnival celebrations to a degree mirror the temperament of their players.

As for other practices and customs peculiar to the festivity, a brief listing includes the Pero Palo (Pete the Stick) of Villanueva de la Vera (Cáceres), a figure that provokes the symbolic ire of the people; the Miel Otxin of Lanz (Navarre), another gigantic straw figure; the *botargas* (devils) and *mascaritas* (masked ones) of Almiruete; the *zarrones*, men disguised as cows, from Atienza (Guadalajara); the *cigarrones* (locusts) in Laza (Orense); the *trangas* (mask with goat skins and large antlers) from Bielsa (Huesca); and the provocative *guirrios* from León.

Once the effigy of Carnival is burned and the sardine is buried and with the onset of Lent, a more or less stable time frame for festivals begins. The celebrations lasting through these days take on a lugubrious nature: night processions, "mortal sin" in the form of a woman in mourning; requests for alms for the souls in purgatory; plaintive trumpet calls, like those of the gigantic *bocinas*, or horns, from Chincilla (Albacete); devout practices of diverse religious brotherhoods. This is a good moment to reflect on past festivals or to prepare for future festivities. The circle of celebration has closed — although, of course, only for the moment.

J. M. Caballero Bonald

THE PHOTOGRAPHS

1. **Los Escobazos** (Festival of the Burning Brooms). Jarandilla (Cáceres)

2. Los Escobazos (Festival of the Burning Brooms). Jarandilla (Cáceres)

3. Los Escobazos (Festival of the Burning Brooms). Jarandilla (Cáceres)

4. La Santantoná (Saint Anthony's Day). Forcall (Castellón)

5. La Santantoná (Saint Anthony's Day). Forcall (Castellón)

6. SAN ANTÓN (Saint Anthony's Day). Villanueva de Alcolea (Castellón)

7. LA OBISPARRA (Mock Bishop's Masquerade): Devils. Riofrío de Aliste (Zamora)

8. La Obisparra (Mock Bishop's Masquerade): The acolyte and the blindman. Riofrío de Aliste (Zamora)

9. NOISEMAKERS. Abejera de Tábara (Zamora)

10. Clown. Montamarta (Zamora)

11. **Clown.** Sanzoles del Vino (Zamora)

12. SAN JULIÁN (Saint Julian's Day): **DANZA DE REYES** (Dance of the Magi). Gulanes (Pontevedra)

13. **SAN ANTÓN** (Saint Anthony's Day): **BLESSING OF THE ANIMALS**. Muro (Mallorca)

14. Las tentaciones de San Antón (the temptations of Saint Anthony). Artá (Mallorca)

15. **CLOWN.** Piornal (Cáceres)

16. El Pino de San Antón (Saint Anthony's Pine Tree). Pollensa (Mallorca)

17. La Tabúa (The Reed-mace Festival): **Day of bread and cheese**. Zarza de Montánchez (Cáceres)

18. Carnival: Bear. Ituren and Zubieta (Navarre)

19. Carnival: El Zampanzar (Festival of Saint Fatbelly). Ituren and Zubieta (Navarre)

20. La Endiablada (Festival of the Bewitched). Almonacid del Marquesado (Cuenca)

21. BOTARGAS DE SAN BLAS (devils of Saint Blas). Albalate de Zorita (Guadalajara)

22. BOTARGA DE LA CANDELARIA (devil of Candlemas). Arbancón (Guadalajara)

23. LAS AGUEDAS (Festival of the Married Women). Peleagonzalo (Zamora)

24. LAS ALCALDESAS (Festival of the Mayors' Wives): Burning of the figure. Zamarramala (Segovia)

25. LAS AGUEDAS (Festival of the Married Women). Miranda del Castañar (Salamanca)

26. PANBENDITERAS (Festival of the Single Women). Escatrón (Teruel)

27. CARNIVAL: THE MASKED ONES. Almiruete (Guadalajara)

28. CARNIVAL. Fuentes de Andalucía (Seville)

29. CARNIVAL: FIESTA DEL MARKITOS (Festival of the *Markitos* Figure). Zalduendo (Alava)

30. CARNIVAL: LOS CARNEROS (Festivity of the Sheep). Frontera (El Hierro)

31. CARNIVAL. Buxan (Orense)

32. CARNIVAL: CIGARRONES (Carnival figures). Laza (Orense)

33. CARNIVAL: BOTEIROS (leapers). Viana do Bolo (Orense)

34. CARNIVAL: LADIES. Cobres (Pontevedra)

35. Carnival: "La Maja Desnuda" ("The Naked Maja"). Ciudad Real

36. CARNIVAL: DIABLETES (little devils). Teguise (Lanzarote)

37. Carnival: Child with sun hat. Viano do Bolo (Orense)

38. CARNIVAL: DISGUISE. San Sebastián (Guipúzcoa)

39. CARNIVAL: CHIRIGOTAS (Festivity of the Jesters). Cádiz

40. CARNIVAL. Arcos de la Frontera (Cádiz)

41. Carnival: Guirrios (Carnival figures). Velilla de la Reina (León)

42. CARNIVAL: VOLANTE (flier). Santiago de Rivas (Lugo)

43. Carnival: Tranga (Carnival figure). Bielsa (Huesca)

44. CARNIVAL. Madrid

45. FALLAS (Festival of the Bonfires). Valencia

46. FALLAS (Festival of the Bonfires): **LA CREMÁ** (the burning). Valencia

47. FALLAS (Festival of the Bonfires): **LA CREMÁ** (the burning). Valencia

48. HOLY WEEK: THE BROTHERHOOD OF THE HOLY CROSS. Seville

49. HOLY WEEK: THE BROTHERHOOD OF CANDLEMAS. Seville

50. HOLY WEEK: THE BROTHERHOOD OF CANDLEMAS. Seville

51. HOLY WEEK, GOOD FRIDAY: PENITENTS OF THE BROTHERHOOD OF HUMILITY. Archidona (Málaga)

52. STATIONS OF THE CROSS. San Vicente de la Sonsierra (La Rioja)

53. LOS COLINEGROS (the blacktails). Baena (Córdoba)

54. Holy Week: Biblical figures. Puente Genil (Córdoba)

55. HOLY WEEK: NAZARENE OF SAINT BENEDICT. Seville

56. HOLY WEEK: THE BROTHERHOOD OF CANDLEMAS. Seville

57. HOLY WEEK: GUIDING CROSS, THE BROTHERHOOD OF PEACE. Seville

58. HOLY WEEK: FLOAT CARRIERS, THE BROTHERHOOD OF SAINT BENEDICT. Seville

59. PROCESIÓN DEL SANTO CRISTO (Procession of the Holy Christ). Bercianos de Aliste (Zamora)

60. Procesión del Santo Entierro (Procession of the Holy Interment). Bercianos de Aliste (Zamora)

61. LOS PICAOS (Procession of the Pierced). San Vicente de la Sonsierra (La Rioja)

112

62. EL EMPALAO (Procession of the Impaled). Valverde de la Vera (Cáceres)

63. HOLY WEEK, GOOD FRIDAY: EL SONIDO DE LA BURLA (the sound of the mocking of Christ). Murcia

64. HOLY WEEK: EL PASO (The Passion). Riogordo (Málaga)

65. Holy Week: El Drama de la Cruz (The Drama of the Cross Festival). Alcorisa (Teruel)

66. HOLY WEEK: EL PASO (The Passion). Riogordo (Málaga)

67. Holy Week: El Paso (The Passion). Riogordo (Málaga)

68. LA PASSIÓ (The Passion). Cervera (Lérida)

69. HOLY WEEK: EL CRISTO DE LOS GITANOS (the Christ of the gypsies). Granada

70. LOS PEREGRINOS (the pilgrims). Useras (Castellón)

71. ROMERÍA DE LA VIRGEN DE LA CABEZA (Pilgrimage of the Virgin of La Cabeza). Andújar (Jaén)

72. Float carriers of the Virgen de la Cabeza. Andújar (Jaén)

73. ROMERÍA DE LA TRINIDAD (Pilgrimage of the Trinity). Lumbier (Navarre)

74. ROMERÍA DE LA VIRGEN DEL CASTILLO (Pilgrimage of the Virgin of El Castillo). Fariza de Sayago (Zamora)

75. Romería de la Virgen de la Peña (Pilgrimage of the Virgin of Sorrow). Puebla de Guzmán (Huelva)

76. Romería de la Virgen de Castrotierra (Pilgrimage of the Virgin of Castrotierra). Castrotierra de la Valduerna (León)

77. **ROMERÍA DE LA VIRGEN DE LAS ALCANTARILLAS** (Pilgrimage of the Virgin of the Bridges). Belalcázar (Córdoba)

78. ROGATIVA DE LLUVIA (Prayer for Rain). Tirteafuera (Ciudad Real)

79. CRUZ DEL ROMERO (Pilgrim's Cross). Bonares (Huelva)

80. LA MAYA (Festival of the May Girl). Colmenar Viejo (Madrid)

81. LAS CRUCES (Festival of the Crosses). El Berrocal (Huelva)

82. LAS CRUCES (Festival of the Crosses). El Berrocal (Huelva)

83. CRUCES DE MAYO (Festival of the May Crosses): EL ROMERO (the pilgrim). Almonaster la Real (Huelva)

84. LA MAYA (Festival of the May Girl). Colmenar Viejo (Madrid)

85. NOCHE DE LOS FAVORES (Festival of the Night of Favors). Alosno (Huelva)

86. Semana Santa Chiquita (Little Holy Week). Puente Genil (Córdoba)

87. **CRUCES DE MAYO** (Festival of the May Crosses). Estepa (Seville)

88. Fiesta de la Santísima y Vera Cruz (Festival of the Most Holy and True Cross). Caravaca (Murcia)

89. FIESTA DE LA SANTÍSIMA Y VERA CRUZ (Festival of the Most Holy and True Cross): **LOS CABALLOS DEL VINO** (the wine horses). Caravaca (Murcia)

90. **Fiestas del Santísimo Cristo de la Agonía** (Festival of the Most Holy Christ of the Agony): **Entrance of the Moorish army.** Onteniente (Valencia)

91. SAINT MICHAEL'S DAY: EL SONADOR (the music maker). San Miguel de Balanzat (Ibiza)

92. DANZANTES DE LA VIRGEN DE LA TÓRTOLA (Dancers of the Virgin of the Turtledove). Hinojosa (Huelva)

93. Danzante del Cristo Arrodillado (Dancer of the Kneeling Christ). Belinchón (Cuenca)

94. Fiesta del Pan Bendito (Festival of the Blessed Bread). Torremanzanas (Alicante)

95. Romería del Rocío (Pilgrimage of El Rocío): Cart driver from Triana. El Rocío (Huelva)

96. ROMERÍA DEL ROCÍO (Pilgrimage of El Rocío): Baptism in the Quema River. El Rocío (Huelva)

97. ROMERÍA DEL ROCÍO (Pilgrimage of El Rocío): Brotherhood from Huelva. El Rocío (Huelva)

98. ROMERÍA DEL ROCÍO (Pilgrimage of El Rocío): Brotherhood from Triana on the Raya Real. El Rocío (Huelva)

99. ROMERÍA DEL ROCÍO (Pilgrimage of El Rocío): Brotherhood from Ecija. El Rocío (Huelva)

100. ROMERÍA DEL ROCÍO (Pilgrimage of El Rocío). El Rocío (Huelva)

101. Romería del Rocío (Pilgrimage of El Rocío): Brotherhood from Jerez de la Frontera, in Lucio de los Ansares (Huelva)

102. Romería del Rocío (Pilgrimage of El Rocío): Pilgrim. El Rocío (Huelva)

103. Romería del Rocío (Pilgrimage of El Rocío): Lucio de los Ansares (Huelva)

104. ROMERÍA DEL ROCÍO (Pilgrimage of El Rocío). El Rocío (Huelva)

105. ROMERÍA DEL ROCÍO (Pilgrimage of El Rocío). El Rocío (Huelva)

106. Romería del Rocío (Pilgrimage of El Rocío). El Rocío (Huelva)

107. Romería del Rocío (Pilgrimage of El Rocío): Procession of the Virgin of El Rocío (Huelva)

108. Traslado de la Virgen del Rocío (Transfer of the Virgin of El Rocío). Almonte (Huelva)

109. Festival of the Virgin of the Incarnation: Devil. El Hito (Cuenca)

110. CORPUS CHRISTI. Camuñas (Toledo)

III. CORPUS CHRISTI: VIRTUDES (virtues). Camuñas (Toledo)

112. Corpus Christi: Pecados (sins). Camuñas (Toledo)

113. LOS CABALLITOS (Festival of the Little Horses). Peñalsordo (Badajoz)

114. EL COLACHO (The Devil). Castrillo de Murcia (Burgos)

115. Danza del Capitán (Captain's Dance). Frías (Burgos)

116. CORPUS CHRISTI. Oñate (Guipúzcoa)

117. CORPUS CHRISTI: MOMA (mummer). Valencia

118. Corpus Christi: Penlas (children of the procession). Rodondela (Pontevedra)

119. CORPUS CHRISTI. Lagartera (Toledo)

120. Saint John's Day: Altars. Sigüenza (Guadalajara)

121. Saint John's Day: Rite. Manacor (Mallorca)

122. CORPUS CHRISTI: PROCESSION. Valencia

123. PASO DEL FUEGO (walking on coals). San Pedro Manrique (Soria)

124. SAINT JOHN'S DAY: BONFIRES. Alicante

125. SAINT JOHN'S DAY. Ciudadela (Menorca)

126. Saint Thecla's Day: Castellers (human towers). Santa Tecla (Tarragona)

127. Saint Felix's Day: Castellers (human towers). Villafranca del Penedés (Barcelona)

128. ELS ELOIS (Saint Eligius's Day). Berga (Barcelona)

129. VIRGEN DEL CARMEN (Festival of the Virgin of Mount Carmel): Procession through the sea. Los Boliches, Fuengirola (Málaga)

130. MOROS Y CRISTIANOS (Moors and Christians Festival): **EL DESEMBARCO** (the landing). Villajoyosa (Alicante)

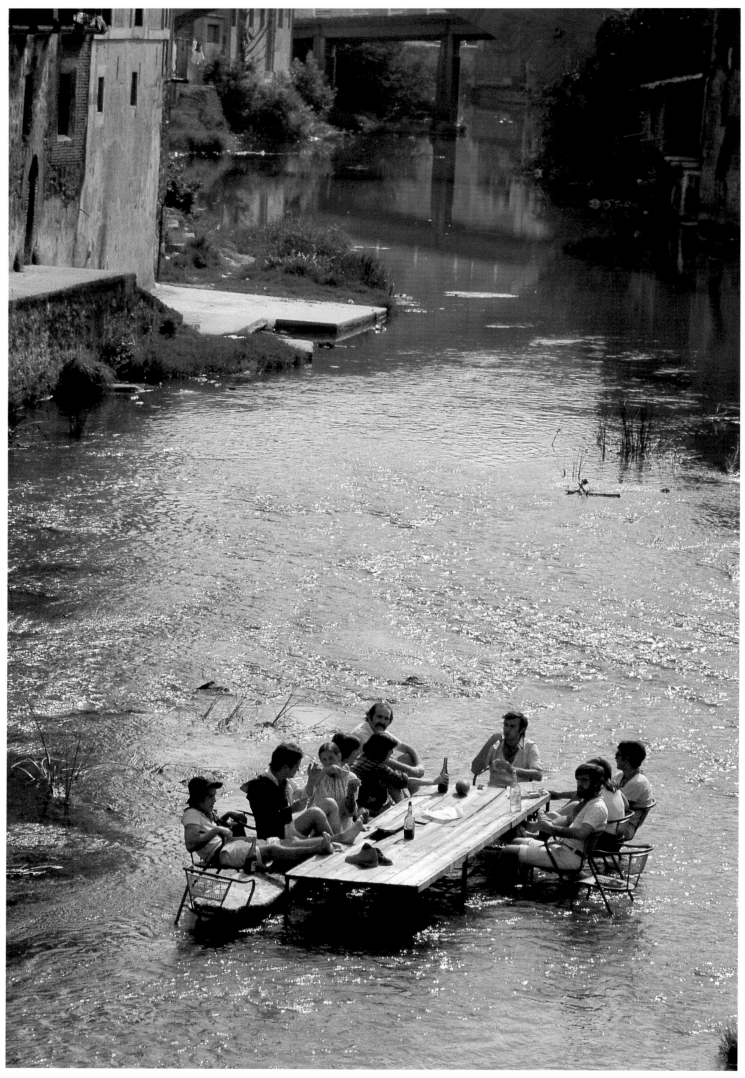

131. Saint Andrew's Day: Almuerzo en el río Ega (lunch in the Ega River). Estella (Navarre)

132. SAN ANTOLÍN (Saint Anthony's Day): **LOS GANSOS** (Festivity of the Geese). Lequeitio (Vizcaya)

133. SAN ADRIÁN DEL MAR (Feast Day of Saint Hadrian of the Sea). Malpica de Bergantiños (La Coruña)

134. ROMERÍA DE LA VIRGEN DE LA BARCA (Pilgrimage of the Virgin of the Boat). Muxía (La Coruña)

135. Romería en el Monte de Santa Tecla (Pilgrimage on Mount Santa Tecla). La Guardia (Pontevedra)

136. ROMERÍA EN EL MONTE DE SANTA TECLA (Pilgrimage on Mount Santa Tecla). La Guardia (Pontevedra)

137. SAINT ANDREW'S DAY: LA PAÑUELADA (Festivity of the Handkerchiefs). Estella (Navarre)

138. LA TOMATINA (The Tomato Battle). Buñol (Valencia)

139. La Tomatina (The Tomato Battle). Buñol (Valencia)

140. Festival of Saint John: Bullfights. Coría (Cáceres)

141. FESTIVAL OF SAINT JOHN: BULLFIGHTS. Coría (Cáceres)

142. Capea (bullfights with young bulls). Garganta la Olla (Cáceres)

143. CAPEA (bullfights with young bulls). Garganta la Olla (Cáceres)

144. Encierro del Pilón (bull run of El Pilón). Falces (Navarre)

145. Saint Fermin's Festival: Encierros (bull runs). Pamplona (Navarre)

146. FESTIVAL OF THE VIRGIN OF THE PILLAR: LAS VAQUILLAS (Festivity of the Heifers). Saragossa

147. La Vaca Ensogada (Festivity of the Roped Cow). Albadalejo (Ciudad Real)

148. LOS SANJUANES (Festival of Saint John): **EL MALETILLA** (the aspiring bullfighter). Coría (Cáceres)

149. FIESTAS DE LA SANTÍSIMA SANGRE (Festival of the Most Holy Blood): TOROS EN EL MAR (bulls in the sea). Denia (Alicante)

150. FIESTAS DE LA SANTÍSIMA SANGRE (Festival of the Most Holy Blood): TOROS EN EL MAR (bulls in the sea). Denia (Alicante)

151. Saint Fermin's Festival: El Kiliki Caravinagre (Vinegar Face). Pamplona (Navarre)

152. Saint Fermin's Festival: Zaldiko (horse figure). Pamplona (Navarre)

153. CURRO DE MORGADANES (Horse Corralling in Santiago de Morgadanes). Gondomar (Pontevedra)

154. Saint Orosia's Day: Pilgrims. Jaca (Huesca)

155. Festival of the Virgin of Davalillo: Dances. San Asensio (La Rioja)

156. CORPUS CHRISTI: SOLDADO DEL SANTÍSIMO (soldier of the Holy Eucharist). Peñalsordo (Badajoz)

157. Costume of La Alberca (Salamanca)

158. Costume of Berga (Barcelona)

159. DÍA DEL TRAJE (Costume Day). Ansó (Huesca)

160. Costume of a Sephardic bride. Madrid

161. GALA COSTUME. La Alberca (Salamanca)

162. MAYORDOMA DE LA VIRGEN DE LA PEÑA (servant of the Virgin of Sorrow). Puebla de Guzmán (Huelva)

163. Romería de San Benito (Pilgrimage of Saint Benedict). Cerro de Andévalo (Huelva)

164. ROMERÍA GITANA (Gypsy Pilgrimage). Fregenal de la Sierra (Badajoz)

165. **SAN SALVADOR** (Holy Savior): **BAJADA DE LA VIRGEN DE LOS REYES** (Descent of the Virgin of the Kings). Hierro Island (Canaries)

166. EL CRISTO DEL PAÑO (The Christ of the Cloth). Moclín (Granada)

167. La Virgen de la Cigüeña (The Virgin of the Stork). Fuente de Saz (Madrid)

168. La Virgen de la Cigüeña (The Virgin of the Stork). Fuente de Saz (Madrid)

169. EL TORO JÚBILO (The Bull with Lit Tar Torches). Medinaceli (Soria)

170. El Cristo del Sahúco (The Christ of El Sahúco). Peñas de San Pedro (Albacete)

171. Romería de Santa Marta (Pilgrimage of Saint Martha). Ribarteme (Pontevedra)

172. Romería del Santo Cristo de la Agonía (Pilgrimage of Holy Christ of the Agony). Gende (Pontevedra)

247

173. ROMERÍA DE SANTA MARTA (Pilgrimage of Saint Martha): **OFRECIDO** (offering). Ribarteme (Pontevedra)

174. ROMERÍA DE SANTA MARTA (Pilgrimage of Saint Martha): **OFRECIDO** (offering). Ribarteme (Pontevedra)

175. **S**ANTO **N**IÑO DE LA **G**UARDIA (Holy Christ Child of La Guardia): Votive offering. La Guardia (Toledo)

176. SAN CAMPIO (Saint Campius's Day). Figueiró (Pontevedra)

177. Saint Minnia's Festival. Brión (La Coruña)

178. La Virgen de los Remedios (The Virgin of the Rosary): **Meco** (devil). La Hermida (Lugo)

179. DÍA DE TODOS LOS SANTOS (All Saints' Day). La Alberca (Salamanca)

180. La Procesión del Humo (The Procession of Smoke). Arnedillo (La Rioja)

181. FIESTA DE ANIMAS (Festival of the Souls in Purgatory): EL ANIMERO MAYOR (the head solicitor). Almedina (Ciudad Real)

182. Day of the Innocents: El blanco (the white penitent). El Ballestero (Albacete)

183. EL VÍTOR (The Cheer). Mayorga de Campos (Valladolid)

184. EL VÍTOR (The Cheer). Mayorga de Campos (Valladolid)

185. EL **V**ÍTOR (The Cheer). Mayorga de Campos (Valladolid)

186. EL VÍTOR (The Cheer). Mayorga de Campos (Valladolid)

187. EL VÍTOR (The Cheer). Mayorga de Campos (Valladolid)

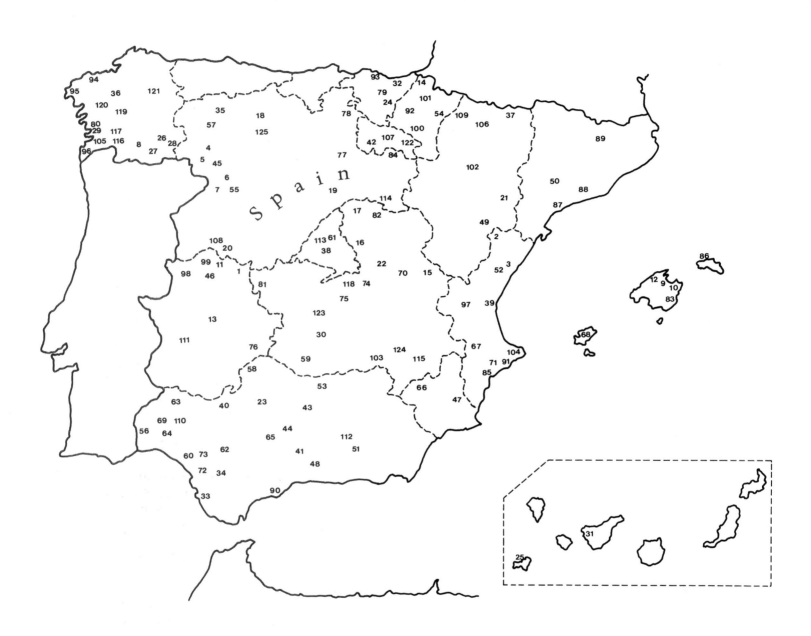

S p a i n

Numbers in **boldface** correspond to those on the map; numbers in *italics* refer to illustration numbers.

1. *1, 2, 3.* Jarandilla, Cáceres.
2. *4, 5.* Forcall, Castellón.
3. *6.* Villanueva de Alcolea, Castellón.
4. *7, 8.* Riofrío de Aliste, Zamora.
5. *9.* Abejera de Tábara, Zamora.
6. *10.* Montamarta, Zamora.
7. *11.* Sanzoles del Vino, Zamora.
8. *12.* Gulanes, Pontevedra.
9. *13.* Muro, Mallorca.
10. *14.* Artá, Mallorca.
11. *15.* Piornal, Cáceres.
12. *16.* Pollensa, Mallorca.
13. *17.* Zarza de Montánchez, Cáceres.
14. *18, 19.* Ituren y Zubieta, Navarre.
15. *20.* Almonacid del Marquesado, Cuenca.
16. *21.* Albalate de Zorita, Guadalajara.
17. *22.* Arbancón, Guadalajara.
18. *23.* Peleagonzalo, Zamora.
19. *24.* Zamarramala, Segovia.
20. *25.* Miranda del Castañar, Salamanca.
21. *26.* Escatrón, Teruel.
22. *27.* Almiruete, Guadalajara.
23. *28.* Fuentes de Andalucía, Seville.
24. *29.* Zalduendo, Alava.
25. *30, 165.* Frontera, El Hierro.
26. *31.* Buxan, Orense.
27. *32.* Laza, Orense.
28. *33, 37.* Viana do Bolo, Orense.
29. *34.* Cobres, Pontevedra.
30. *35.* Ciudad Real.
31. *36.* Teguise, Lanzarote.
32. *38.* San Sebastián, Guipúzcoa.
33. *39.* Cádiz.
34. *40.* Arcos de la Frontera, Cádiz.
35. *41.* Velilla de la Reina, León.
36. *42.* Santiago de Rivas, Lugo.
37. *43.* Bielsa, Huesca.
38. *44, 160.* Madrid.
39. *45, 46, 47, 117, 122.* Valencia.
40. *48, 49, 50, 55, 56, 57, 58.* Seville.

41. *51.* Archidona, Málaga.
42. *52, 61.* San Vicente de la Sonsierra, La Rioja.
43. *53.* Baena, Córdoba.
44. *54, 86.* Puente Genil, Córdoba.
45. *59, 60.* Bercianos de Aliste, Zamora.
46. *62.* Valverde de la Vera, Cáceres.
47. *63.* Murcia.
48. *64, 66, 67.* Riogordo, Málaga.
49. *65.* Alcorisa, Teruel.
50. *68.* Cervera, Lérida.
51. *69.* Granada.
52. *70.* Useras, Castellón.
53. *71, 72.* Andújar, Jaén.
54. *73.* Lumbier, Navarre.
55. *74.* Fariza de Sayago, Zamora.
56. *75, 162.* Puebla de Guzmán, Huelva.
57. *76.* Castrotierra de la Valduerna, León.
58. *77.* Belalcázar, Córdoba.
59. *78.* Tirteafuera, Ciudad Real.
60. *79.* Bonares, Huelva.
61. *80, 84.* Colmenar Viejo, Madrid.
62. *81, 82.* El Berrocal, Huelva.
63. *83.* Almonaster la Real, Huelva.
64. *85.* Alosno, Huelva.
65. *87.* Estepa, Seville.
66. *88, 89.* Caravaca, Murcia.
67. *90.* Onteniente, Valencia.
68. *91.* San Miguel de Balanzat, Ibiza.
69. *92.* Hinojales, Huelva.
70. *93.* Belinchón, Cuenca.
71. *94.* Torremanzanas, Alicante.
72. *95, 96, 97, 98, 99, 100, 101, 102, 103, 104, 105, 106, 107.* Huelva.
73. *108.* Almonte, Huelva.
74. *109.* El Hito, Cuenca.
75. *110, 111, 112.* Camuñas, Toledo.
76. *113, 156.* Peñalsordo, Badajoz.
77. *114.* Castrillo de Murcia, Burgos.
78. *115.* Frías, Burgos.
79. *116.* Oñate, Guipúzcoa.
80. *118.* Redondela, Pontevedra.
81. *119.* Lagartera, Toledo.
82. *120.* Sigüenza, Guadalajara.
83. *121.* Manacor, Mallorca.
84. *123.* San Pedro Manrique, Soria.
85. *124.* Alicante.

86. *125.* Ciudadela, Menorca.
87. *126.* Tarragona.
88. *127.* Villafranca del Penedés, Barcelona.
89. *128, 158.* Berga, Barcelona.
90. *129.* Fuengirola, Málaga.
91. *130.* Villajoyosa, Alicante.
92. *131, 137.* Estella, Navarre.
93. *132.* Lequeitio, Vizcaya.
94. *133.* Malpica de Bergantiños, La Coruña.
95. *134.* Muxía, La Coruña.
96. *135, 136.* La Guardia, Pontevedra.
97. *138, 139.* Buñol, Valencia.
98. *140, 141, 148.* Coria, Cáceres.
99. *142, 143.* Garganta la Olla, Cáceres.
100. *144.* Falces, Navarre.
101. *145, 151, 152.* Pamplona, Navarre.
102. *146.* Saragossa.
103. *147.* Albadalejo, Ciudad Real.
104. *149, 150.* Denia, Alicante.
105. *153.* Gondomar, Pontevedra.
106. *154.* Jaca, Huesca.
107. *155.* San Asensio, La Rioja.
108. *157, 161, 179.* La Alberca, Salamanca.
109. *159.* Ansó, Huesca.
110. *163.* Cerro de Andévalo, Huelva.
111. *164.* Fregenal de la Sierra, Badajoz.
112. *166.* Moclín, Granada.
113. *167, 168.* Fuente el Saz, Madrid.
114. *169.* Medinaceli, Soria.
115. *170.* Peñas de San Pedro, Albacete.
116. *171, 173, 174.* Ribarteme, Pontevedra.
117. *172.* Gende, Pontevedra.
118. *175.* La Guardia, Toledo.
119. *176.* Figueiró, Pontevedra.
120. *177.* Brión, La Coruña.
121. *178.* La Hermida, Lugo.
122. *180.* Arnedillo, La Rioja.
123. *181.* Almedina, Ciudad Real.
124. *182.* El Ballestero, Albacete.
125. *183, 184, 185, 186, 187.* Mayorga de Campos, Valladolid.

EXPLANATORY NOTES
TO THE PHOTOGRAPHS

1, 2, and 3. LOS ESCOBAZOS (Festival of the Burning Brooms). Jarandilla (Cáceres). December 7 and 8

On the evening of December 7 all the townspeople put on old clothes for a "battle" of fire. Beside numerous bonfires built on streets and squares, people prepare *escobones*, or large brooms—some of them over six feet long. After lighting these brooms, participants strike each other, amid a hail of sparks. When the brooms are almost consumed, the procession begins, accompanying the banner of the Virgin Mary through the streets of Jarandilla, as centuries-old hymns relating to the Immaculate Conception are sung.

4 and 5. LA SANTANTONÁ (Saint Anthony's Day). Forcall (Castellón). January 16 and 17 or the following weekend

Sometimes the life of this saint is dramatized in the main square. The *santantoná* begins at nightfall on January 16, with a procession in which the figures of Saint Anthony and Saint Paul appear, tied by the hands and dragged on a rope pulled by *El Despullat* (the naked man). Also present is *La Filoseta,* a man dressed as a woman representing the saint's temptations of the flesh, as well as *botargas,* hooded devils attired in white garb covered with drawings of toads and snakes. Armed with clubs, they beat both the ground and the spectators and attempt to scale balconies and pursue members of the opposite sex. The *cremaller,* or lighter, sets fire to the *barraca,* a type of Valencian cabin made of dry branches and brushwood through which devils run, leaping and shouting. The festivity ends with the feigned death of the saint inside the *barraca.*

6. SAN ANTÓN (Saint Anthony's Day). Villanueva de Alcolea (Castellón). January 16 or the following Saturday

At dusk, the municipal officials or festival arrangers, on horseback, leap over innumerable bonfires started throughout the town.

7 and 8. LA OBISPARRA (Mock Bishop's Masquerade). Riofrío de Aliste (Zamora). January 1

A winter masquerade in which citizens seek to bury the old year and welcome the new year, the *obisparra* is composed of *carochos,* large and small devils carrying pincers tipped with the horns of a he-goat, five *guapos* (gallants), and four *filandorros* (spinners), who form the comical part of the festivity. The performances take place during the morning on all the streets of the town.

9. NOISEMAKERS. Abejera de Tábara (Zamora). January 1

The *cencerrón,* or noisemaker, with his large pincers, pursues neighbors while the *filandorra* (spinner) throws ashes on the spectators. Other figures are the *gitano* (gypsy), who, dressed in multicolored garb, rides a burro, and the *ciegos* (blind men), who recite satirical verses on the year's events in the town.

10. CLOWN. Montamarta (Zamora). January 1 and 6

A *quinto* (recruit), wearing a cork mask and a colorful costume and carrying a trident and cowbells at his waist, goes around the town asking for his Epiphany gift as he pursues the men of the neighborhood. The *zangarrón,* or clown, does not enter the church until the conclusion of the mass. Then he enters, his mask removed, to present before the altar his offering of two loaves of bread. On January 1 he wears a black mask and on the sixth he wears a red one.

11. CLOWN. Sanzoles del Vino (Zamora). December 26

The *zangarrón,* or clown, goes through the streets asking for his Epiphany gift and running after youths and children, whom he threatens with the large pig bladders he carries in his hands. At the same time he sounds the cowbells he carries on his back. Accompanying him are the year's recruits who, following the church service, will dance in the main square before the image of Saint Stephen.

12. SAN JULIÁN (Saint Julian's Day): **DANZA DE REYES** (Dance of the Magi). Gulanes (Pontevedra). January 6

Three couples interpret straw, arch, and ribbon dances, accompanied by bagpipe music. In Galician, these dances are known as Ranchos dos Reis.

13. SAN ANTÓN (Saint Anthony's Day): **BLESSING OF THE ANIMALS.** Muro (Mallorca). January 17

The animals are blessed to protect them from sickness.

14. LAS TENTACIÓNES DE SAN ANTÓN (the temptations of Saint Anthony). Artá (Mallorca). January 16 and 17

The *dimonis*, or devils, comprise the principal figures, who devote their energies to "tormenting" the saint. The night before (that is, January 16), bonfires are lit and people sing and drink "Saint Anthony's cocoa" in front of the flames. On January 17 the townsfolk celebrate the procession with animals and carts representing scenes from the life of Saint Anthony.

15. CLOWN. Piornal (Cáceres). January 19 and 20

In this penitential masquerade in honor of Saint Sebastian, the *jarramplas*, or clown, wearing a horned mask and playing a drum, goes through the streets of the town for two days. He sports a multicolored costume, fully lined to protect him from the rain of turnips and snowballs hurled at him by his neighbors.

16. EL PINO DE SAN ANTÓN (Saint Anthony's Pine Tree). Pollensa (Mallorca). January 17

Youths of the town select and cut down a tall pine tree in Ternelles. Once it is stripped of its bark the tree is transported for several miles—in about three hours—to the old main square, where it is erected. Then the revelers cover two-thirds of the trunk with soap and try to climb it in order to reach the prizes hung at the top.

17. LA TABÚA (The Reed-mace Festival): **DAY OF BREAD AND CHEESE.** Zarza de Montánchez (Cáceres)

When the inhabitants emerge from mass and reach the arcades, they throw *tabúas*, or reed-mace, aquatic plants that were gathered from the banks of the Guadiana River. Then the town council offers bread and goat cheese.

18 *and* 19. CARNIVAL: EL ZAMPANZAR (Festival of Saint Fatbelly). Ituren and Zubieta (Navarre). Monday and Tuesday after the last Sunday in January

The first day in Ituren and the next in Zubieta, the *zampanzar*, or Carnival figures, proceed through the town and countryside. Each wears a *tunturro*, a cone-shaped, multicolored cap topped with ribbons, two huge cowbells, petticoats, sheepskins, and carries a *hisopa*, or small broom. In one of the neighborhoods they will pick up the enormous *oso*, or bear, held on a chain by a masked figure who serves as a trainer.

20. LA ENDIABLADA (Festival of the Bewitched). Almonacid del Marquesado (Cuenca). February 2 and 3

The townsmen, dressed as devils, gather before the house of the head devil in order to accompany the statue of the Virgin of Candlemas on a procession. During the two days of the festivities, they ring constantly the enormous cowbells they carry on their backs, as they run races and leap before the religious figures.

21. BOTARGAS DE SAN BLAS (devils of Saint Blas). Albalate de Zorita (Guadalajara). February 3

Drinking wine, dancing, and hailing Saint Blas, the *botargas*, or devils, accompany the saint's image as they attempt to halt the advancing procession. The religious brotherhood in charge of organizing the festivity distributes *caridades*, or small loaves of bread, and once they are blessed they are eaten to protect the throat from illness.

22. BOTARGA DE LA CANDELARIA (devil of Candlemas). Arbancón (Guadalajara). February 2 or the first Sunday of February

The *botarga*, or devil, wanders through the streets asking for his Epiphany gift and chasing the neighborhood youths.

23. LAS AGUEDAS (Festival of the Married Women). Peleagonzalo (Zamora). February 5

After a procession around the church in which the married women carry the image of Saint Agatha covered with embroidered silk shawls, three young men emerge in antique attire and plumed hats, carrying long staffs. These individuals confront the townspeople, who try to break their staffs.

24. LAS ALCALDESAS (Festival of the Mayors' Wives). Zamarramala (Segovia). The Sunday following February 5

To celebrate Saint Agatha's Day, each year the town of Zamarramala elects two mayors' wives, who preside over the festivities and govern the town for this day. During the procession they are accompanied by the *águedas*, or married women, dressed as farmers. Then they burn a dummy, the symbol for a man, and perform such traditional dances as the Wheel Dance. The costumes of these mayors' wives are the most luxurious in the province of Segovia.

25. LAS AGUEDAS (Festival of the Married Women). Miranda del Castañar (Salamanca). February 5

Attired in traditional costumes and wearing family jewels, the *águedas* wander through the town, reciting songs in honor of Saint Agatha. At the conclusion, each one, beginning with the bailiff's wife, "dances" the flag over her husband, who remains lying at her feet.

26. PANBENDITERAS (Festival of the Single Women). Escatrón (Teruel). February 5

One hour before the procession of the blessed bread, the gathering of the bread is held at ten o'clock. In the procession, the *panbenditeras*, or single women, wearing the exquisite costume typical of the Escatrón farm woman, march accompanied by men with shotguns.

27. CARNIVAL: THE MASKED ONES. Almiruete (Guadalajara)

The site where the townsfolk dress is kept a secret. The men (*botargas*, or devils) hide behind cardboard masks of bright colors. The women (*mascaritas*) disguise themselves with silk masks. The devils carry cowbells to frighten off spirits as well as a staff, the symbol of the shepherd. They proceed through the town three times in a row.

28. CARNIVAL. Fuentes de Andalucía (Seville)

Groups of masked people go through the streets during the three days of Carnival and Piñata Sunday, the first Sunday of Lent, when a ceramic pot filled with sweets is broken by a blindfolded person with a stick. They alter their voices so as not to be recognized by their neighbors.

29. CARNIVAL: FIESTA DEL MARKITOS (Festivity of the *Markitos* Figure). Zalduendo (Alava). Carnival Sunday

Everything revolves around the *markitos*, a puppet that is taken around the town in a cart and then placed atop a pole in front of the church. After being subjected to a trial, he is burned on Sunday afternoon. Other characters in this ceremony are the *vieja*, or old woman (who in reality represents a man "riding" an old woman), sheep, the bear, the shepherd, the ash sellers, and the *zampantzas* (Carnival figures) stuffed into sacks filled with straw, who keep shoving each other around in the streets.

30. CARNIVAL: LOS CARNEROS (Festivity of the Sheep). Frontera (El Hierro)

Youths disguise themselves with sheepskins (*zaleas*), placing on their heads a wicker basket forming a sheep's head with horns and painting their face, arms, and legs black. Then they run after young boys and girls.

31. CARNIVAL. Buxan (Orense)

Several figures accompanied by a *folión,* or musical group, visit neighboring villages. In this festival, all the traditional elements of the age-old rural carnival appear: the bear, the sheep, the cart for performing the farce, masks, and the *meco*, or devil, hung on balconies, to be burned or torn up on the last day of the celebration.

32. CARNIVAL: CIGARRONES (Carnival figures). Laza (Orense). Sunday, Monday, and Tuesday of Carnival

Sporting enormous, flashy masks, the *cigarrones,* or Carnival figures, pursue townsfolk with their whips. They go through the town as a group for three days, ringing the huge cowbells they wear on their backs. On Monday morning, the battle of the *farrapos* (rags smeared with mud) takes place. In the afternoon, members of the *morena* (a man with a cow's head) group throw flour and ants at the spectators. The festival concludes late Tuesday, the "great day," with the reading of the "burro's last will and testament."

33. CARNIVAL: BOTEIROS (leapers). Viana do Bolo (Orense). Sunday and Monday of Carnival

As Viana is the commercial center for the region, on Sunday the *foliones,* or musical groups, arrive from all the neighboring villages, playing an odd assortment of percussion instruments, such as pots, frying pans, spoons. Of particular note during the main procession are the *boteiros,* or leapers. Wearing enormous masks decorated with colored crepe paper and brandishing long polelike sticks, as they go through the streets they execute tremendous leaps.

34. CARNIVAL: LADIES. Cobres (Pontevedra). Sunday, Monday, and Tuesday of Carnival

The Carnival of Cobres takes place in the parishes of Saint Hadrian and Saint Christina. The procession is formed by *madamas* (ladies) and *galanes* (gallants) wearing large hats adorned with flowers, ribbons, mirrors, and jewels. For three days the group goes around the town, dancing at the doorways of houses, where they are invited to partake of beverages and sweets.

35. CARNIVAL: "LA MAJA DESNUDA" ("The Naked Maja"). Ciudad Real

The majority of the Carnival *peñas*, or groups, of the principal neighboring villages around Ciudad Real participate in the great procession held in the capital. The different *peñas* perform scenes that recall figures from *Don Quixote* to those from famous paintings, such as this version of a work by Francisco de Goya.

36. CARNIVAL: DIABLETES (little devils). Teguise (Lanzarote)

The *diabletes*—figures whose origins can be found in the festivals of Corpus Christi—cover their faces with masks adorned with long red tongues and horns. They carry a goatskin game bag, with which they beat spectators.

37. CARNIVAL: CHILD WITH SUN HAT. Viano do Bolo (Orense)

Sunday of Carnival, the inhabitants arrive for the procession in Viana with their *foliones*, or musical groups.

38. CARNIVAL: DISGUISE. San Sebastián (Guipúzcoa)

In San Sebastián—as in many other places—the disguises of Carnival include the themes of gender change and transvestism: men become women, and women transform themselves into men. The festival begins on Saturday with a public declaration and the reception for the Momus, the Greek god of mockery, before the town hall and ends with a massive *entierro de la sardina*, or burial of the sardine.

39. CARNIVAL: CHIRIGOTAS (Festivity of the Jesters). Cádiz

Choruses, quartets, and jesters perform in the streets and squares of Cádiz during Carnival week, from Carnival Sunday to Piñata Sunday.

40. CARNIVAL. Arcos de la Frontera (Cádiz)

Couples, groups, and individuals march through the streets wearing disguises, mostly homemade.

41. CARNIVAL: GUIRRIOS (Carnival figures). Velilla de la Reina (León). Carnival Sunday

In the afternoon, after the rosary mass, *guirrios* and *toros* (bulls), youths in disguise who pursue the girls, appear on the streets of the town. Then the "bulls" charge the *guirrios*, who try to evade them. The *guirrio* wears an enormous cardboard mask, complete with a colored rosette; he is dressed in white with a folded handkerchief as a sash belt. These figures make young girls leap over the horns of the "bulls."

42. CARNIVAL: VOLANTE (flier). Santiago de Rivas (Lugo)

Attired with a long plume and hundreds of multicolored ribbons that are not supposed to touch the ground, the *volante* goes around leaping and ringing the bells on his waistband. This Carnival figure solicits charitable contributions at doorways and, in the afternoon, performs "holy offices," parodies, and comic satires.

43. CARNIVAL: TRANGA (Carnival figure). Bielsa (Huesca)

With their antlers, little balls, and long staffs, with which they strike the ground, the twenty-odd *trangas*, or Carnival figures, form a striking contrast with the *madamas*, or ladies, the other protagonists of this Pyrenees festivity. Beside them the *amuntato*, a man "riding" an old woman, and figures of bears, a horse, and the shepherdesses run and leap through the streets.

44. CARNIVAL. Madrid

A great cavalcade and the *entierro de la sardina*, or burial of the sardine, are the principal practices of the Madrid Carnival, happily reinstituted. The participants reveal a great creativity and sense of humor in the preparation of masks and costumes. The "Joyful Fraternity of the Holy Interment" and the professional wailers dressed in strict mourning attire have renewed an age-old tradition by which Carnival receives its farewell.

45, 46, 47. FALLAS (Festival of the Bonfires). Valencia. March 19

The most important days of this festival are March 18, with the offering of flowers to the Virgen de los Desamparados (Virgin of the Forsaken), and the following day—Saint Joseph's Day—which begins with the *despertá*, or awakening. At noon the *mascletá*, a noisy assembly with colored smoke, fireworks, and firecrackers, takes place. At nightfall revelers hold the *cremá*, or cremation (in which all the figures will be burned), and set off fireworks. Only one *ninot* (a figure of a little boy), the best one, will be spared from the flames.

48, 49, 50, 55, 56, 57, 58. HOLY WEEK. Seville

The religious brotherhoods are in charge of bringing splendor to Semana Santa, or Holy Week, in Seville. Each one traditionally sponsors several sculpted floats featuring the Virgin and a scene of the Passion of Christ. The procession is the same for all the brotherhoods: Nazarenes, wearing tunics with different colors to represent different brotherhoods, accompany the float, which is transported by the *costaleros*, or float carriers, on its course through the streets of the city. The most exciting moments are when the floats exit from and enter the church, as members of the crowd break out into *saetas*, spontaneous popular songs of a religious nature.

51. HOLY WEEK: PENITENTS OF THE BROTHERHOOD OF HUMILITY. Archidona (Málaga). Good Friday

Friday is the main day of Holy Week. In the morning the popular *niño de la bola* (Christ child of the ball) is borne through the streets. In the afternoon the floats of Jesús de la Humildad (Jesus of Humility) and María Santísima de los Dolores (Our Lady of Sorrows) are carried through the streets. At night the floats of the Holy Sepulcher and Our Lady of Solitude are carried through the town. The penitents wear a hood, a crown of thorns, and a cross.

52. STATIONS OF THE CROSS. San Vicente de la Sonsierra (La Rioja). Sunday after May 3 and September 4

On these days of the cross, flagellants known as *picaos* (pierced) take part on a route of the Stations of the Cross toward Calvary.

53. HOLY WEEK: COLIBLANCOS Y COLINEGROS (Whitetails and Blacktails). Baena (Córdoba)

During the course of Holy Week, the uninterrupted drumrolls played by the so-called *judíos* (Jews) resound through the streets. These participants are divided into two *turbas*, or groups. The *coliblancos* wear helmets with white horsehair tails; the *colinegros* wear helmets with black tails. There is also a procession of apostles, evangelists, executioners, and Roman centurions with masks, and a religious drama is staged.

54. HOLY WEEK: BIBLICAL FIGURES. Puente Genil (Córdoba). Good Friday

Figures from the Old and New Testaments as well as allegorical figures participate in this festivity. Theological plays are also performed. Everyone marches with a *rastrillo*, or mask covering his face. Beside them march "soldiers" from the Roman Empire. Each group or religious brotherhood features its *alpatana*, or wine steward, so no one lacks for wine during the long procession.

59 and 60. HOLY WEEK. Bercianos de Aliste (Zamora). Holy Thursday and Good Friday

On Holy Thursday the Stations of the Cross procession is held, when the men wear heavy, dark capes from the town of Alcañices. On Friday, for the procession of the Holy Interment, members of the religious brotherhoods wear white robes. At the end of the Passion sermon that very afternoon, the figure of a jointed, crucified Christ is detached from the wall and placed in a glass case. The processional cross, banners of the brotherhoods, and penitents accompany the figure on a procession through the field toward the crosses of Calvary.

61. LOS PICAOS (Procession of the Pierced). San Vicente de la Sonsierra (La Rioja). Holy Thursday and Good Friday, and Sundays after Cross Sunday in May and September

The flagellants, barefoot and their faces covered so as not to be recognized, whip their backs with knots of linen until blisters form. Then the *práctico*, or practitioner, pierces the blisters to draw blood.

62. EL EMPALAO (Procession of the Impaled). Valverde de la Vera (Cáceres). Holy Thursday

At nightfall on Holy Thursday, some of the inhabitants "impale" themselves to fulfill some promise. This harsh penitence consists of binding the body and the outstretched arms to a small tree trunk with a tight rope. Then the penitents don a crown of thorns, cover their faces with a veil, cross two sharpened sabers on their backs, and proceed through the town on a path of the Stations of the Cross, guided by both a relative to light their way with an oil lamp and the *cireneo*, or assistant, to help them.

63. HOLY WEEK. Murcia. Good Friday

Among the rituals of Holy Week in Murcia are people carrying Baroque figures by Francisco Salzillo, a Spanish sculptor who lived from 1707 to 1783, on their shoulders, as well as Nazarenes with their puffed-out habits laden down by the weight of the caramel candies they distribute during the processions. Among the sounds are songs at dawn, untuned drums, and *bocinas*, long trumpets that produce mocking sounds, representing the mocking of Christ.

64, 66, and 67. EL PASO (The Passion). Riogordo (Málaga). Good Friday and Easter Sunday

The town itself serves as a setting for the open-air staging of the Lord's Passion, with the inhabitants playing the lead roles. Almost all the actors are country folk who have rehearsed their roles for several weeks.

65. HOLY WEEK: EL DRAMA DE LA CRUZ (The Drama of the Cross Festival). Alcorisa (Teruel)

Christ's difficult ascent to the summit of Calvary with a tree trunk on his back is, along with the Crucifixion, the most impressive act of this living Passion, celebrated at 5 P.M. on Good Friday.

68. LA PASSIÓ (The Passion). Cervera (Lérida). Sundays during Lent, Holy Week, and following

The staging of the Cervera Passion drama, the oldest in Catalonia, dating back to the fifteenth century, lasts the whole day. Some three hundred characters participate in this performance with thirty-six scenes, held in an enclosed space.

69. HOLY WEEK: EL CRISTO DE LOS GITANOS (the Christ of the gypsies). Granada. Holy Wednesday

At night, a Christ figure begins the ascent to the hill of Sacromonte. The gypsies await him at the foot of their caves with bonfires and torches to dedicate *saetas,* spontaneous popular songs of a religious nature, to him. The crucified Christ, his silhouette profiled against the flames and the Alhambra, will take the whole night to reach the abbey of Sacromonte.

70. LOS PEREGRINOS (the pilgrims). Useras (Castellón). Last Friday and Saturday in April

A dozen men preceded by a guide, all with full beards and wearing purple habits and hats, symbolize the twelve apostles and Christ. Accompanied by a priest, keeper of the keys, and singers, they depart from the church of Useras at dawn on Friday on a long pilgrimage to the hermitage of San Juan de Penyagolosa, praying as they go along the route. In this way they fulfill a promise made to the saint who saved the town from a series of epidemics.

71 and 72. ROMERÍA DE LA VIRGEN DE LA CABEZA (Pilgrimage of the Virgin of La Cabeza). Andújar (Jaén). Last Saturday and Sunday in April

More than fifty religious brotherhoods from all over Andalusia participate in this pilgrimage on horseback, mule, and on foot. The procession leaves Andújar Saturday morning to cover the eighteen miles to the sanctuary of the Virgen de la Cabeza, on the mountain peak. At night the whole town resounds with the clapping of hands and hymns in the space between improvised booths and the bonfires. On Sunday the statue of the Virgin emerges, carried on the shoulders of the devout, amid shouts, cheers, and tears.

73. ROMERÍA DE LA TRINIDAD (Pilgrimage of the Trinity). Lumbier (Navarre). Trinity Sunday

At eight in the morning, the *cruceros,* or cross bearers, barefoot on this procession, begin their ascent to the hermitage located on the summit of the hill. On their arrival, an open-air mass is held, and then they descend. At the entrance to the town, a priest goes out to meet them with a processional cross.

74. ROMERÍA DE LA VIRGEN DEL CASTILLO (Pilgrimage of the Virgin of El Castillo). Fariza de Sayago (Zamora). First Saturday and Sunday in June

This pilgrimage to the sanctuary of the Virgin of El Castillo is accompanied by parish crosses, figures of Christ, and *viriatos,* white banners representing the towns in the district. Each banner measures some seven and a half yards and features on top some holm oak branches, out of which emerge the *vientos,* or ropes, that serve to control it.

75. ROMERÍA DE LA VIRGEN DE LA PEÑA (Pilgrimage of the Virgin of Sorrow). Puebla de Guzmán (Huelva). Last Sunday in April

To fulfill a vow of thanksgiving for the Virgin's having saved the town from a plague in the seventeenth century, pilgrims ride on horseback to the sanctuary of the Virgen de la Peña. Here they hold a procession with her statue and dance sword dances in her honor.

76. ROMERÍA DE LA VIRGEN DE CASTROTIERRA (Pilgrimage of the Virgin of Castrotierra). Castrotierra de la Valduerna (León). Variable date in May

The supplication for rain is celebrated every seven years or in a time of drought. The *procuradores de la tierra* (solicitors of the earth) decide when the Romanesque statue of the Virgin is to be taken out. The transfer takes place through the fields, as the Virgin, along with huge banners and parish crosses, makes the eleven-mile trip from the sanctuary to the Astorga cathedral. She remains there for nine days, after which the statue is again borne in pilgrimage back to the sanctuary.

77. ROMERÍA DE LA VIRGEN DE LAS ALCANTARILLAS (Pilgrimage of the Virgin of the Bridges). Belalcázar (Córdoba). Last Sunday in April

After a vigil to the Virgin in the light of bonfires at the hermitage of Monterrubio, the procession of the statue leaves for Belalcázar before daybreak. The most exciting moment is when the procession crosses the Zújar River, the pilgrims bearing the statue of the Virgin on their shoulders in the middle of the current in a supplication for rain. As the procession reaches Belalcázar at nightfall, the statue is greeted with lighted torches.

78. ROGATIVA DE LLUVIA (Prayer for Rain). Tirteafuera (Ciudad Real). May 1

On the eve of the festival, May songs are sung to the Virgin of the Rosary. On the first of May, inhabitants leave the town of Villamayor on a procession with the statue to Tirteafuera, a journey of five miles. They stop at the estate of La Cruz to have a breakfast of fried breadcrumbs and then continue across the river with the statue of Saint Joseph. The carriers, who have taken a vow to participate, enter the waters as they pray for rain for the fields with hymns and prayers.

79. CRUZ DEL ROMERO (Pilgrim's Cross). Bonares (Huelva). Third Saturday and Sunday in May

There are twelve crosses, one for each religious brotherhood. Every year one of these takes charge of organizing the festivities, which are kept secret. Saturday morning after mass, people ride on horseback from the chapel of the Pilgrim's Cross to a nearby spot, where a lunch is served. On Sunday there is a procession, and participants bow reverentially to the crosses of the Pilgrim's Cross.

80 and 84. LA MAYA (Festival of the May Girl). Colmenar Viejo (Madrid). May 2

At 4 in the afternoon, several *mayas* wearing petticoats and white dresses, embroidered silk shawls, necklaces, and floral adornments are placed on the May altar. Each *maya* must remain silent and motionless for some three hours, until a jury decides which one is the best. Meanwhile, the attendants, comb in hand, "comb" the passersby for contributions, placed in a dish in front of the *maya*.

81 and 82. LAS CRUCES (Festival of the Crosses). El Berrocal (Huelva). May 1–4

This festival, with a pilgrimage, a procession, and dances, centers on the *mozos de la bandera*, or flag youths, a young man and woman who are in charge of offering the pilgrim to the crosses. The latter are adorned with flowers, mirrors, and gold and silver jewels.

83. CRUCES DE MAYO (Festival of the May Crosses). Almonaster la Real (Huelva). First Saturday and Sunday in May

Two rival religious brotherhoods, each directed by a man and a woman, prepare the crosses. On Saturday, the "Day of Flowers," the branches, plants, and flowers for decorating the crosses are gathered. On Sunday the procession takes place; at its conclusion each brotherhood sings and lays a bouquet of rosemary at the cross of its rival.

85. NOCHE DE LOS FAVORES (Festival of the Night of Favors). Alosno (Huelva). First and second Saturday in May

May crosses are decorated for this festival, and a *hermana mayor* (head nun) on each street takes charge of the expenses. The women in each neighborhood sing fandangos and dance *sevillanas* (Sevillian dances) in front of their cross on the "night of favors," the culmination of the festival.

86. SEMANA SANTA CHIQUITA (Little Holy Week). Puente Genil (Córdoba). May 1–3

This three-day May festival corresponds to Holy Wednesday and Thursday and to Good Friday (the most important day). The difference is that the participants are children and the size of the floats they carry in the procession—of biblical figures, exact copies of the larger ones—is smaller.

87. Cruces de Mayo (Festival of the May Crosses). Estepa (Seville)

The day of the cross has its greatest expression in Andalusia. Rare indeed is the town or village that does not celebrate the festival. Little is needed: a cross—of wood or flowers—and a group that sings or dances or simply gathers to chat in front of it. Children also decorate crosses with flowers and prepare small Holy Week floats that they carry through the streets.

88 *and* 89. Fiesta de la Santísima y Vera Cruz (Festival of the Most Holy and True Cross). Caravaca (Murcia). May 1–5

On May 2 a mass commemorating the apparition of the cross is held. The festival's most spectacular events are the procession and the *carrera de los caballos de vino*, or race of the wine horses, in which the animals are richly adorned. In the climb to the castle, the horses are held by the bridle and led at a run, thus recalling an episode in the battles between Arabs and Christians.

90. Fiestas del Santísimo Cristo de la Agonía (Festival of the Most Holy Christ of the Agony): **Moros y Cristianos** (Moors and Christians Festivities). Onteniente (Valencia). Last Friday, Saturday, and Sunday in August

Friday is the day of the entrance of the armies, first the Christian and then the Moorish. Saturday afternoon the Descent of Christ is celebrated, and at night there are fireworks.

91. Saint Michael's Day: El sonador (the music maker). San Miguel de Balanzat (Ibiza). September 29

This festivity in honor of Saint Michael the archangel, patron saint of the town, includes a procession and traditional wedding dances, like Sa Curta and Sa Llarga (The Short and The Long in Mallorcan), to the accompaniment of the music maker playing on the flute and drum.

92. Danzantes de la Virgen de la Tórtola (Dancers of the Virgin of the Turtledove). Hinojosa (Huelva). May 1

After high mass, a procession bearing the statue of the Virgin leaves the church. The Dance of the Turtledove is performed on this day in her honor, to the beating of a small drum.

93. Danzante del Cristo Arrodillado (Dancer of the Kneeling Christ). Belinchón (Cuenca). Sunday following the Ascension (fortieth day after Easter)

The procession is in honor of the Most Holy Kneeling Christ. Eight young dancers with starched white petticoats dance on the route, led by the *castañolón* (castanet player), dressed in green and red, who uses a large castanet for begging alms. Also present is the *porra* (cudgel carrier).

94. Fiesta del Pan Bendito (Festival of the Blessed Bread). Torremanzanas (Alicante). May 9 and the second Sunday of May

In honor of Saint Gregory, who saved the town from a plague of locusts, a procession of *clavariesas* (bread bearers) is held after a visit to the cemetery. These girls, wearing white costumes, carry a loaf of bread weighing some seventeen pounds or so, decorated with fresh flowers, on their heads. A *custodi* (guardian), a family member or friend, accompanies each girl.

95–107. Romería del Rocío (Pilgrimage of El Rocío). El Rocío (Huelva). Saturday, Sunday, and Monday of Pentecost

Andalusia's most popular pilgrimage is attended by more than a million persons. Of these, some sixty thousand make the journey with one of the more than seventy religious brotherhoods. On Saturday, these pilgrims parade before the Virgin of El Rocío and are received by the principal brotherhood in Almonte. In the wee hours of Monday morning, the inhabitants of Almonte "leap over the railing" and carry the Virgin out, bearing her on a procession through the town.

108. TRASLADO DE LA VIRGEN DEL ROCÍO (Transfer of the Virgin of El Rocío). Almonte (Huelva). Month of August

Every seven years a huge procession takes the statue of the Virgin of El Rocío to Almonte on a night in August, depending on the date for Pentecost. The Virgin, attired as a shepherdess and covered to protect her from the dust, is carried over the nine and a half miles that separate El Rocío and Almonte. The procession traditionally arrives at dawn, when the statue is uncovered and borne through the streets of the town, where it will remain until Pentecost.

109. FESTIVAL OF THE VIRGIN OF THE INCARNATION: DIABLOS Y DANZANTES (devils and dancers). El Hito (Cuenca). May 28

In honor of the Virgin of the Incarnation, participants in this procession transport her statue for a mile and a half, accompanied by devils and dancers. First it stops at a site known as La Mesa, where the statue was discovered hidden. Stick dances are performed there, the fields are blessed, and participants return with blessed pastry rings.

110–12. CORPUS CHRISTI. Camuñas (Toledo). Corpus Christi and the following Sunday

Two religious brotherhoods take part in a liturgical drama between *los pecados* and *las virtudes* (the sins and the virtues). After mass, a procession is held and the Dance of the Virtues, in which souls are redeemed, is performed. Then one at a time, the figures of the sins run out shouting and kneel before the host.

113. LOS CABALLITOS (Festival of the Little Horses). Peñalsordo (Badajoz). Corpus Christi week

This celebration commemorates a battle with the Moors. In the morning, members of the religious brotherhood, adorned with paper flowers, ride on donkeys to the outskirts of the town, where young bulls charge them. Afterward, all meet at the house of the head brother to attend mass, then they go on a procession. They end up in front of the church, where they build a "human tower." Every four years, they also carry out the festivity called *alcancías de los caballitos*, a dance in which the brothers throw hundreds of eggs filled with sawdust at the spectators.

114. EL COLACHO (The Devil). Castrillo de Murcia (Burgos). Midweek of Corpus Christi

In this festivity, which dates back to 1621, the image of the Corpus Christi is carried through the streets. The babies born during the year are placed on mattresses laid on the streets of the procession. Two people known as *colachos*, representing the devil, leap over these newborn. It is popularly believed that as a result of these leaps, evil will leave their bodies and the children will be spared illness.

115. DANZA DEL CAPITÁN (Captain's Dance). Frías (Burgos). Sunday nearest June 24

Captain's dances are performed during festivities of Saint John the Baptist by four dancers dressed in white petticoats and colored silk handkerchiefs.

116. CORPUS CHRISTI. Oñate (Guipúzcoa). Sunday following Corpus Christi

Saint Michael, Jesus, and the twelve apostles, their faces covered with masks, go along the town's streets on a procession. They are accompanied by flute players and dancers who play and dance before the Eucharist, processional crosses, and children taking their First Communion who throw rose petals, as well as the monstrance beneath a canopy.

117 and 122. CORPUS CHRISTI. Valencia. Sunday after Corpus Christi

The *moma*, or mummer, who represents virtue, attired in white and her face covered, dances a traditional dance beside the *momos*. Giants and dwarfs also dance, and there is a procession of Old Testament figures, eagles, a dragon and other mythological animals, as well as *rocas* (triumphal floats).

118. CORPUS CHRISTI: PENLAS (children of the procession). Rodondela (Pontevedra). Sunday after Corpus Christi

This festival includes sword dances and the Danza Gremial de las Penlas (Guild Dance of the Penlas), in which two women dressed in white (*burras*) balance on their heads a *penla*, or little girl dressed like an angel, as they dance on a carpet of flower petals before the Eucharist.

119. CORPUS CHRISTI. Lagartera (Toledo). Sunday after Corpus Christi

This town, famous for its embroidery, places its best work on balconies, streets, and altars to honor the Eucharist. As the figure of Christ passes, the newborn, lying on these embroidered cloths, are blessed.

120. SAINT JOHN'S DAY: ALTARS. Sigüenza (Guadalajara). June 24

Children prepare altars on the streets and squares with the figure of Saint John and seek alms from passersby. At night bonfires are lit.

121. SAINT JOHN'S DAY: RITE. Manacor (Mallorca). June 24

As dawn breaks on Saint John's Day, naked children are passed between the branches of a special tree, the *vimet*, or osier, to cure them of hernias. Then the parents tie the cut branches with ribbons.

123. PASO DEL FUEGO (walking on coals). San Pedro Manrique (Soria). June 23

On the night of June 23, barefoot men walk over a carpet of burning coals, carrying a person on their back. People say that the weight of the person chosen and the manner of walking are what keep the participants from getting burned.

124. SAINT JOHN'S DAY: BONFIRES. Alicante. June 23

The culmination of the *nit del foc*, night of fire in Valencian, follows the fireworks, when revelers light the bonfires with figures that—just as in Valencia—were specially made to be consumed on this night. There is a simultaneous rain of rockets.

125. SAINT JOHN'S DAY. Ciudadela (Menorca). June 23–24 and the prior Sunday

The *caixer senyor* (a master of ceremonies), a noble, invites the representatives of the city's estates to honor Saint John in his hermitage and celebrate a medieval tournament, during which a rigid protocol is observed. The *jaleos* (Andalusian dances) provide the high point of the festivity, when the horses, to the accompaniment of music, leap amid the enthusiastic celebrators, who hold them back with their hands.

126. SAINT THECLA'S DAY: CASTELLERS (human towers). Santa Tecla (Tarragona). September 23

The *castellers* rise in front of the cathedral and, delicately balanced, proceed down the main street as far as the town hall, where the young boy crowning this human tower is raised to the balcony of the building.

127. SAINT FELIX'S DAY: CASTELLERS (human towers). Villafranca del Penedés (Barcelona). August 3

In one of Catalonia's most dangerous and representative traditions, *collas* (groups) erect human towers several stories high, crowned with a little boy known as the *anxareta* (little goose).

128. ELS ELOIS (Saint Eligius's Day). Berga (Barcelona). The Sunday following July 25

Saint Eligius is the patron saint of muleteers. The riders participating in the festivity ride through the streets—where they get a splashing from above—to the Plaza de Santa Magdalena, where berries and *barreja* (a beverage made with brandy and wine) are distributed. Then they go to another square, where the animals are blessed. Finally, a mass is celebrated in which blessed bread is given out.

129. VIRGEN DEL CARMEN (Festival of the Virgin of Mount Carmel). Los Boliches, Fuengirola (Málaga). July 16

At eight at night the statue of the Virgen del Carmen emerges from the church on the shoulders of the sailors to be taken through the town and to the beach promenade. They enter the waters of the sea with the statue, which protects them from danger. They are followed by groups of the faithful, who carry candles. Fishermen with their decorated boats approach and illuminate the statue and sound their foghorns.

130. MOROS Y CRISTIANOS (Moors and Christians Festival). Villajoyosa (Alicante). July 28–29

Bursting fireworks, rockets, firecrackers, and musical bands lend sound to the episode of the Arab landing that is repulsed, thanks to the protection of Saint Martha. Moors and Christians "fight" on the beach and in the water, following several parade reviews, embassies, attacks, and counterattacks.

131 *and* 137. SAINT ANDREW'S DAY. Estella (Navarre). First Sunday in August

Saint Andrew's Day has a procession of figures of dwarfs and giants, dancers, the running of bulls, offerings, and the *pañuelada*, as hundreds of people wave red handkerchiefs in front of the town hall. In some years, young men place tables and chairs in the Ega River to eat lunch.

132. SAN ANTOLÍN (Saint Anthony's Day): **LOS GANSOS** (Festivity of the Geese). Lequeitio (Vizcaya). September 5

The festivities, including Saint Anthony's Day, last the whole week. Several geese are hung upside down from a rope tied between the masts from two ships in the port. Bands of young boys in small boats pass underneath and try to decapitate the birds by hanging from their necks.

133. SAN ADRIÁN DEL MAR (Feast Day of Saint Hadrian of the Sea). Malpica de Bergantiños (La Coruña). July 16, if it falls on a Sunday; otherwise, the following Sunday

The statue of Saint Hadrian is borne on the participants' shoulders, first along the beach, then up the mountain, from the parish church of Malpica to its hermitage, on the cape of San Adrián. The faithful wear long, colored ribbons attached on one end to the saint. At the conclusion an auction is held and the offerings are sold.

134. ROMERÍA DE LA VIRGEN DE LA BARCA (Pilgrimage of the Virgin of the Boat). Muxía (La Coruña). The Sunday after September 8

On the pilgrimage to the sanctuary of the Virgen de la Barca, pilgrims traditionally pass nine times under the *pedra dos cadres* (the kidney stone in Galician) in order to become cured of backaches. They also go up to the *pedra de abalar* (the moving stone) to try to move it in a demonstration of strength.

135 *and* 136. ROMERÍA EN EL MONTE DE SANTA TECLA (Pilgrimage on Mount Santa Tecla). La Guardia (Pontevedra). Second Sunday in August

Against a background of one of Galicia's most beautiful panoramas, youths celebrate this festivity by engaging in a "wine battle" and dancing to the rhythm of the *troulada*, music of bagpipes and bass drums.

138 *and* 139. LA TOMATINA (The Tomato Battle). Buñol (Valencia). Last Wednesday in August

Some fifty-five tons of tomatoes, brought on trucks to the main square, are used in this bloodless battle in honor of the patron saint of Buñol, in which ripe tomatoes are thrown in a free-for-all. Afterward, with the help of hoses, all pitch in to ensure the town's return to its normal aspect.

140 and 141. FESTIVAL OF SAINT JOHN: BULLFIGHTS. Coría (Cáceres). Around June 24

After playing with death in the running of the bulls, participants approach the just killed bull (the most powerful, dangerous, and admired animal in their world) to touch it close up. In the festivities of bull runs or bullfights with young bulls in the streets and squares, it is necessary to extract the dead animal's blood immediately so that the meat will not spoil and can be sold for food. This bull meat can serve to make cauldrons of stew, of which the whole town can partake.

142 and 143. CAPEA (bullfights with young bulls). Garganta la Olla (Cáceres). July 2–4

A religious celebration is held on July 2, while on the third and fourth, the protagonist is the bull. The bullfighting enclosure is built from tree trunks in the beautiful main square, but the main refuge is always the stone fountain, where youths fleeing from the animal's charges huddle.

144. ENCIERRO DEL PILÓN (bull run of El Pilón). Falces (Navarre). From the second until the third Sunday in August

This is a spectacular run of young bulls over some thousand feet, down the mountain on a curving slope, which makes this one of the most original and dangerous of runs. It is held each day of the week-long festival at nine in the morning.

145, 151, and 152. SAINT FERMIN'S FESTIVAL. Pamplona (Navarre). July 7–14

During this week the most famous and crowded runs in Spain are held. They take place every day at 8 A.M. After the run, the young bulls are turned loose in the bullring. The *kilikis* (giant-headed figures) and other figures are very popular with the children.

146. FESTIVAL OF THE VIRGIN OF THE PILLAR: LAS VAQUILLAS (Festivity of the Heifers). Saragossa. October 12

Among the festivities in honor of the Virgen del Pillar held during the week of October 12 is that of the heifers (although young bulls are actually used), which are turned loose in the bullring. Here the originality is that the youths, grouped together at the entrance of the ring, where the animals emerge, endure the charges without moving.

147. LA VACA ENSOGADA (Festivity of the Roped Cow). Albadalejo (Ciudad Real). July 24–25

On the morning of July 24, a rope is hooked on the horns of a bull, and youths pull the young bull through the town while evading its charges. When the animal is exhausted, it is led to a stone fountain, in which the kids also end up.

148. LOS SANJUANES (Festival of Saint John). Coría (Cáceres). June 23–30

Each day during the Festival of Saint John, the walls of the old part of the city are blocked off and a bull is let loose. First it is fought in the main square before the town hall by youths and aspiring bullfighters. With the third signal of the bell, the square is opened and the animal runs free through the streets of the town. The doors of the houses must remain open to offer protection to those in danger from the bull's horns.

149 and 150. FIESTAS DE LA SANTÍSIMA SANGRE (Festival of the Most Holy Blood): **TOROS EN EL MAR** (bulls in the sea). Denia (Alicante). Second Sunday in July

The main part of the Festival of the Most Holy Blood, which also includes climbing greased poles, flower combats, and carriages, is the *bous,* or bulls, that are "fought" all week long in the port area. Participants escape from them by jumping into the sea, and they try to make the bulls fall into the waters.

153. CURRO DE MORGADANES (Horse Corralling in Santiago de Morgadanes). Gondomar (Pontevedra). Third Sunday of June

The wild horses living in freedom on the mountain during the year are brought down to town on this date for the shearing of their manes (*rapa das bestas*) and the branding of their young.

154. SAINT OROSIA'S DAY. Jaca (Huesca). June 25

The evening before the feast day of Saint Orosia, patron saint of Jaca, pilgrims wearing their brown capes and bearing parish crosses arrive from their respective villages. On June 25 a procession is held on the streets of the town, during which the *bandera* (flag dance) and the paloteo (stick dance) are performed. At the conclusion the saint's relics are displayed.

155. FESTIVAL OF THE VIRGIN OF DAVALILLO: DANCES. San Asensio (La Rioja). First week in September

On Saturday and Sunday, the dancers of the Virgin of Davalillo perform *paloteos*, or stick dances. On Monday the pilgrimage is celebrated with a high mass at the hermitage of Davalillo.

156. CORPUS CHRISTI: SOLDADO DEL SANTÍSIMO (soldier of the Holy Eucharist). Peñalsordo (Badajoz)

The uniform of members of the Brotherhood of the Holy Eucharist during the festivities of the week of Corpus Christi.

157 *and* 158. COSTUMES OF LA ALBERCA (Salamanca) **AND BERGA** (Barcelona)

The costume of La Alberca, normally worn daily until recently, is now saved for holidays. The Catalonian farmer of Berga wears this outfit on holidays.

159. DÍA DEL TRAJE (Costume Day). Ansó (Huesca). Last Sunday in August

This celebration honoring Ansó's regional dress has been held since 1976. The female costume of the religious brotherhood traditionally features colored ribbons, rosettes, tresses adorned with ribbons, and ruffs and puffs on the sleeves.

160 *and* 161. COSTUME OF A SEPHARDIC BRIDE (Madrid) **AND GALA COSTUME OF LA ALBERCA** (Salamanca)

The Sephardic bride may wear this outfit in weddings of the Jewish community. The gala costume of La Alberca is worn at weddings and on August 15. One of the most elaborate costumes in all Spain, only four complete sets made of velvet remain. The cape is attached at the waist with a thread belt, and a sash with a large tassel is placed on top. Completing the costume are red stockings and low-heeled black shoes with silver buckles. The shawl is rectangular, made of silk. The most important element is the jewelry, especially the necklaces that reach below the knees. These are made of cylindrical pieces of silver and coral and feature many hanging crosses, reliquaries, and silver fish.

162. MAYORDOMA DE LA VIRGEN DE LA PEÑA (servant of the Virgin of Sorrow). Puebla de Guzmán (Huelva). Last Sunday in April

The costume worn by this servant in the festival of the Virgen de la Peña is made of velvet. The blouse is white, with embroidered sleeves, and the vest has decorations on the back. On her head she wears a lace shawl topped with a hat with plumes and wrought-gold jewels.

163. ROMERÍA DE SAN BENITO (Pilgrimage of Saint Benedict). Cerro de Andévalo (Huelva). First Sunday in May, the previous Saturday, and the following Monday, Tuesday, and Wednesday

This pilgrimage has been celebrated since the sixteenth century. On Saturday a procession journeys to the sanctuary, arriving at dusk. On Sunday the *lanzadores* (throwers) perform sword dances honoring the saint. Notable are the costumes of the female servant and her retinue, the *jamugueros*, so-called for the *jamugas*, or saddles, on the horses they ride.

164. ROMERÍA GITANA (Gypsy Pilgrimage). Fregenal de la Sierra (Badajoz). Last Sunday in October

Since the 1970s, gypsy families from all over Spain and Portugal have gathered each year in front of the sanctuary of the Virgin of the Rosary, their patron saint, to fulfill promises, dance, sing, and eat together.

165. SAN SALVADOR (Holy Savior): **BAJADA DE LA VIRGEN DE LOS REYES** (Descent of the Virgin of the Kings). Hierro Island (Canaries). July 6, every fourth year

Every four years, pilgrims carry on their shoulders the statue of the Virgen de los Reyes over the twenty-five miles of difficult, dusty roads from the town of Sabinosa to Valverde, the capital of the island, making this one of the longest pilgrimages in Spain. Along the way, more than one hundred dancers, wearing white costumes and hats topped with feathers, perform.

166. EL CRISTO DEL PAÑO (The Christ of the Cloth). Moclín (Granada). October 5

An enormous painting known as *El Cristo del Paño*, an object of great devotion in the area because of its miraculous cures, is carried down the steep slopes from the church, situated at the top of the town, to the fervent cheers of the faithful. Its name derives from the fact that the ailment most often cured was cataracts, in former times known as the illness of the cloth.

167 and 168. LA VIRGEN DE LA CIGÜEÑA (The Virgin of the Stork). Fuente de Saz (Madrid). September 6

At nightfall, when the statue is brought out of the church, the dry stubble in the fields is set ablaze, giving the impression that the Virgen de la Cigüeña (which means stork, a bird that traditionally builds its nest in church belltowers) is walking between the flames.

169. EL TORO JÚBILO (The Bull with Lit Tar Torches). Medinaceli (Soria). Saturday following November 13

At 11 P.M. a bull is brought into the bullring and tied to a post with rope. Its body is covered with clay mud and a contraption with two tar torches is placed on its head. These are subsequently lit. The most dangerous moment is that of cutting the rope to free the bull, which chases the bravest around the ring. The only illumination is provided by five bonfires that are lit in commemoration of the Cuerpos Santos (Holy Bodies), the five patron saints of the town. When the fire goes out the ritual ends, and the bull is returned to the corrals.

170. EL CRISTO DEL SAHÚCO (The Christ of El Sahúco). Peñas de San Pedro (Albacete). Pentecost Monday and August 28

The Christ of El Sahúco, placed in a wooden case, is carried in a run over some nine miles by youths dressed in white who take turns transporting the image. On Pentecost Monday it is taken to the church of Peñas de San Pedro, and it is brought back to the sanctuary on August 28.

171, 173, and 174. ROMERÍA DE SANTA MARTA (Pilgrimage of Saint Martha). Ribarteme (Pontevedra). July 29

This is one of the few places remaining in Galicia where people hold a procession with coffins to offer thanks for having escaped some grave illness. Traditionally, they go around the hermitage on their knees and place banknotes on the saint's mantle.

172. ROMERÍA DEL SANTO CRISTO DE LA AGONÍA (Pilgrimage of Holy Christ of the Agony). Gende (Pontevedra). Saturday and Trinity Sunday

This Galician pilgrimage features votive offerings, penitences, offerings, and a procession in which some pilgrims whose lives have been saved thanks to Christ's intercession carry their coffins as a sign of gratitude.

175. SANTO NIÑO DE LA GUARDIA (Holy Christ of La Guardia). La Guardia (Toledo). September 27

As the figure of Christ is transferred to the hermitage of Santo Niño in La Guardia, the faithful leave wax arms, legs, and heads, among other objects, as votive offerings of gratitude for the cure of their ailments or the granting of some other favor.

176. SAN CAMPIO (Saint Campius's Day). Figueiró (Pontevedra). July 30 or following Sunday

The saint's statue, surrounded by flowers and votive offerings of wax, is taken out on procession. The faithful pass handkerchiefs and objects over the saint's body. In the past some of the devout would present as an offering their own weight in wheat.

177. SAINT MINNIA'S FESTIVAL. Brión (La Coruña). September 26–27

On these days, many faithful from all over Galicia come to ask favors of this martyr, whose relics were brought just over a hundred year ago to Brión by an immigrant. The case containing the saint's remains, as well as the garments covering her, date from 1906. The promises made include going through the church on one's knees, votive offerings of wax figures in the shape of the sick body, or candles to be consumed before the altar. There are also holy cards to request her protection.

178. LA VIRGEN DE LOS REMEDIOS (The Virgin of the Rosary): **MECO** (devil). La Hermida (Lugo). September 8–9

On the pilgrimage of the Virgin of the Rosary, the *meco*, a devil with a red costume and a wooden mask, opens a path for the procession with gorse branches he carries in his hand. The Virgin is also accompanied by the *pamponigas*, or giants. At the conclusion, the *meco* will dance and collect the coins thrown to him by the crowd.

179. DÍA DE TODOS LOS SANTOS (All Saints' Day). La Alberca (Salamanca). November 1

Participants of the procession recite the Rosary on route to the cemetery, situated on the outskirts of town, where the priest offers prayers for the dead over their tombs, especially adorned with flowers for the occasion.

180. LA PROCESIÓN DEL HUMO (The Procession of Smoke). Arnedillo (La Rioja). November 30

The figure of Saint Andrew is passed through the smoke arising from bonfires on which branches of rosemary and savin have been placed. The ceremony commemorates the deliverance from an epidemic centuries ago through the intercession of this saint. In the afternoon, the image of Saint Andrew is carried to his hermitage, this time without any smoke.

181. FIESTA DE ANIMAS (Festival of the Souls in Purgatory). Almedina (Ciudad Real). December 28

The head *animero*, or solicitor for the souls in purgatory, attired in a cap and an outfit of bright colors from which cowbells hang, goes through the town, door by door, offering the cross to be kissed and collecting alms in a woolen sack. With the money collected he offers masses for the souls in purgatory.

182. DAY OF THE INNOCENTS: EL BLANCO (the white penitent). El Ballestero (Albacete). December 28

The morning of the Day of the Innocents, a penitent goes out, dressed in white, and with his face covered he proceeds through the streets. This he does as a promise. Without being seen, he must take a small bell from the altar of the Virgin Mary. On his shoulder he carries a saddlebag to collect alms for masses for the souls in purgatory.

183–87. EL VÍTOR (The Cheer). Mayorga de Campos (Valladolid). September 27

The origin of this civic procession in honor of Saint Toribius of Mogrovejo goes back to the torch-lit reception of the saint's relics by his fellow countrymen on their arrival at night from far-off Peru. Since then, when the date arrives, all the inhabitants, carrying burning wineskins tied on poles, go through the streets on the eve of the saint's day. At the conclusion of the festivity, all the skins are burned in front of the hermitage as all pray a Salve Regina to the Virgin Mary and sing a hymn to the saint.

CRISTINA GARCÍA RODERO

BIOGRAPHY

1949   Born October 14 in Puertollano, Ciudad Real, Spain.

1968-72 Studies painting, receiving an M.F.A., at the University of Madrid.

1969   Begins her studies in photography at the university.

1970-71 Studies photography at the Madrid School of Applied Arts and Artistic Professions.

1971   Receives a scholarship from the Ministry of Education and Science to pursue landscape studies at the painters' residence at El Paular, Segovia. Awarded the bronze medal in the El Paular exhibition of works by scholarship recipients.
Receives a scholarship from the Castellblanch Art Endowment, Barcelona, for advanced study at the State Institute of Art, Florence, Italy.

1972   Studies education at the Institute of Educational Sciences, University of Madrid.

1973   Begins her work on Spanish popular festivals, traditions and customs.
Receives a scholarship in the visual arts from the Juan March Foundation, Madrid.

1974-86 Teaches at the Madrid School of Applied Arts and Artistic Professions.

1980   Receives a scholarship in the visual arts for research in new forms from the Ministry of Culture, Madrid.

1981   Wins the position of Professor of Drawing in Fine Arts (Painting Section), University of Madrid.

1983   Begins to teach photography at the Faculty of Fine Arts, University of Madrid.

1985   Appointed to the Chair of Photography, Schools of Visual Arts and Design.
Awarded the Planeta Prize for Photography for her photographic oeuvre.

1988   Named Best Photographer of the Year, *Foto profesional*, Madrid.

1989   Begins her work on the project "Traditional life, festivals, customs and rituals in the European Mediterranean."
Awarded the prize for the best photography book at the Twentieth International Photography Conference at Arles, France.
Awarded the Eugene Smith Prize for Humanistic Photography, New York.

Named Best Photographer of the Year, *Foto profesional*, Madrid.
Awarded the prize for the best book of the year, *Foto Profesional*, Madrid.
Awarded the "Correo del Arte" Annual Prize for Plastic Arts to the best artist in the field of photography, Madrid.

1990   Awarded the Dr. Erich Salomon Prize, German Photography Association, Cologne.
Awarded the Kodak Photo Book Prize, Stuttgart.

1991   Named Best Photographer of the Year, *Foto profesional*, Madrid.

1993   Wins the position of professor of the University School, University of Madrid.
World Press Photo, first prize in the art section.
Golden Eye Trophy, Amsterdam.

SOLO EXHIBITIONS

1984   "Traditional Festivals in Spain," Mexican Council of Photography, Mexico City.

1985   "Religious Practices in Mediterranean Countries," International Photography Conference, Montpellier, France (cat.).

"Focus 85," Fine Arts Council, Madrid (cat.).

1986   Second Photography Meeting of San Prudencio, Alava Provincial Savings Bank, Vitoria, Spain.

1987   "Images from Spain," Paul Klepper Art Center, Queens College, Flushing, New York.

1988   "Four Spanish Photographers," Center for Creative Photography, University of Tucson, Arizona (cat.).

"Saa dos Peiraos," Vigo, Spain (cat.).

1989   "Hidden Spain," Spanish Museum of Contemporary Art, Madrid (cat.).

Municipal Exhibition Palace, Alfonso Pavilion, La Coruña, Spain.

Nicéphore Nièpce Museum, Chalon-sur-Saône, France.

"Human Very Human," Archbishop's Palace, Twentieth International Photography Conference, Arles, France.

1990   Photo-Fest 90, George R. Brown Convention Center, Houston, Texas.

"The Mediterranean: The Dazzling Light," Fifth Photography Conference, Cathedral Gallery, Carcassonne, France.

Fourth Convention for Images, Exhibition Hall, Tibaes Monastery, Braga, Portugal.

"Hidden Spain," André Malraux Médiathèque, Tourcoing, France.

Photographic Forum, Frankfurt, Germany.

Solleric Palace Exhibition Hall, Palma de Mallorca, Spain.

Canaries Savings Bank Exhibition Hall, Santa Cruz de Tenerife, Spain.

Photographers' Gallery, London.

Jovellanos Museum, Municipal Culture, Gijón, Spain.

Focale, Nyon, Switzerland.

II Diaframma, Milan, Italy.

Reckermann Gallery, Photokina, Cologne, Germany.

Landesbildstelle of Württemberg, Center for Audiovisual Media, Stuttgart, Germany.

Munich City Museum, Germany.

1991   "Hidden Spain," Provincial Museum of Archaeology, Albacete, Spain.

Provincial Museum, Ciudad Real, Spain.

Alonso Ojeda Gallery, Cuenca, Spain.

Cultural Centre, Puertollano (Ciudad Real), Spain.

Palace of the Prince, Guadalajara, Spain.

Court of the Schools, University of Salamanca, Spain.

"Imagina," School of Applied Arts and Artistic Professions, Almería, Spain.

Embarcadero Palace, Santander, Spain.

Seattle Art Museum, Washington, USA.

1992   "Europe. The South," Arco IFEMA, Madrid.

Maritime Council Chamber, Burgos Provincial Government Building, Burgos, Spain.

Municipal Museum, Orense, Spain.

The Byzantine Wall Gallery, Cartagena Town Hall, Cartagena (Murcia), Spain.

Town Hall Gallery, Pamplona, Spain.

"Spain: Festivals and Rituals," Visa pour l'Image 92, Fourth International Festival of Photographic Reporting, Perpignan, France.

1993   Spanish and Dutch Photography. Foto Biennale Enschede.

"Hidden Spain." The Gallery of Contemporary Photography, Santa Monica.

"Spain: Festivals and Rituals." National Museum of Anthropology, Madrid.

GROUP EXHIBITIONS

1974   Institute of Hispanic Culture, Madrid. (cat.).

1975   Third Photo Exhibit, Architects Association, Lérida, Spain.

Tambor Gallery, Madrid. (cat.).

Virreina Palace, Barcelona, Spain.

1976   College of Fine Arts of San Fernando, Madrid.

Exhibition of Spanish Photography, Multitud Gallery, Madrid.

Second Exhibition of Plastic Arts Scholarship Recipients, Juan March Foundation, Madrid. (cat.).

University Photography from Madrid, Photographic Society of Guipúzcoa, San Sebastián, Spain.

1979   Exhibition of the First Photography Conference in Andalusia, Málaga, Spain.

1980   "Spanish Photography Week," Guadalajara, Spain.

The Photography Gallery, Cardiff, U.K.

"New Spanish Photography," Night Gallery, London.

1981   "Thirteen Contemporary Spanish Photographers," House of Photography, Mexican Photography Council, Mexico City.

1982   "Thirteen Contemporary Spanish Photographers," Fuji Gallery, São Paulo, Brazil.

"Arteder," International Exhibition of Graphic Work, Bilbao, Spain (cat.).

1983   "259 Images: Contemporary Photography in Spain," Fine Arts Circle, Madrid. (cat.).

"Contemporary Spanish Photographers," College of Fine Arts, University of Florida, Gainesville, Florida.

"Teachers' Exhibition," Faculty of Fine Arts, University of Madrid.

Arco 83 Exhibition, Redor Gallery, Madrid.

1984   "Contemporary Spanish Photographers," Ohio State University, Ohio.

Thirteen Contemporary Spanish Photographers, House of the Americas, Havana, Cuba.

"The Culture of Castilla-La Mancha and its Roots," Velázquez Palace, Madrid.

1985   "Photography in the Museum," Spanish Museum of Contemporary Art, Madrid.

"Aspects of Spain," Europalia 85. Spain, Hasselt Cultural Center, Belgium.

"Contemporary Spanish Photography," University Art Museum, University of New Mexico, Albuquerque.

"From Europe," Municipal Theater Photogallery, San Martín, Buenos Aires, Argentina.

"Photographs from Spain," Photographic Collection in Folkwang Museum, Essen, Germany (cat.).

"Fifty Years of Colour: Kodachrome 1935-1985," Fine Arts Circle, Madrid.

"Lands, Peoples and Rituals," L'Art, Barcelona, Spain.

1986   "A Women's Thing," Madrid City Hall and Chamberí Municipal Board, Spain.

1987   "After Franco," Marcuse Pfeiffer Gallery, New York.

"Galicia a pé de foto," Alfonso Pavilion, La Coruña, Spain.

1988   Arco Exhibition, Redor Gallery, Madrid.

"Sefarad: Jewish Roots in Spain," Bernard Hilken Gallery, Los Angeles.

Third Photo Biennial, Vigo, Spain.

1989   "Twelve Photographers in Twelve Towns of Europe," Ministry of Agriculture and Forests, France.

"The Photographic Beach," International Conference on Photography and the Audivisual, Montpellier, France.

"Spanish Artists in Europe," Waino Aalronem Museum, Finland (cat.).

1990   Kvindemueet i Danmark, Frauen Museum, Bonn, Germany.

"Last Looks," Alhambra Palace, Granada, Spain.

"The Unknown South," Cultural Center, Utrera, Spain.

"Gandía and La Safor: The Landscapes of Joanot Martorell," Ducal Palace, Gandía, Spain.

First International Exhibition of Photography, Salamanca-90, Salamanca, Spain.

"Vanishing Spain," Photography Gallery, Santa Monica College, Los Angeles.

1991   "Vanishing Spain," International Center of Photography, New York. Saint Anselm College, Manchester, New Hampshire.

"Gandía and La Safor: The Landscapes of Joanot Martorell," Julio González IVAM Center, Valencia, Spain.

"Here and Now," Isabel II Canal Exhibition Center.

"Spanish Artists in Europe," Museum of Modern Art, Paris.

Stejdelik Museum, Amsterdam.

San Ambrogio Museum, Milan.

Museum of Contemporary Art, San Marino.

"The Myth of Eugene Smith: Photographer-Heirs to a Humanistic Tradition," Georges Pompidou Center, Paris.

"The Legacy of Eugene Smith: Twelve Photographers in the Humanistic Tradition." International Center of Photography, Midtown, New York.

"Four Directions in Contemporary Spanish Photography," National Museum, Queen Sofia Art Centre, Madrid.

1992   "Open Spain," The Museum of Contemporary Photography, Chicago.

Botanical Garden, Madrid.

Provincial Museum of Fine Arts, Huelva, Spain.

Lozoya Tower, Segovia, Spain.

Parpalló Hall, Provincial Authority Building, Valencia, Spain.

Centre for the Technology of the Image, University of Málaga, Spain.

Exhibition Hall, Caixa Galicia Foundation, La Coruña, Spain.

"Vanishing Spain," Artists' Loft at Sealy, Galveston.

University of Alabama, Birmingham.

Sinclair Community College, Dayton.

"Spanish Artists in Europe," Barbican Center, London.

Gulbenkian Foundation, Lisbon.

Virreina Palace, Barcelona.

"Shipyards Through Time," Spanish Museum of Contemporary Art, Madrid.

Cádiz Museum.

El Dique History Museum, Puerto de Santa María.

El Born Market, Barcelona.

"Imagine. A Project on Photography." Almediterránea-92, Arenal Gallery.

Spanish Pavilion Expo-92. Maestranza Palace, Seville, Spain.

"Four Directions: Spanish Contemporary Photography 1970-90," School of Arts and Crafts, Almería, Spain.

Sa Nostra Center, Palma de Mallorca, Spain.

Ste. Anne's Church, Montpellier, France.

Louisiana Museum, Humlebaeck, Denmark.

Pallarés Cultural Center, León, Spain.

University Exhibition Hall, Santander, Spain.

Almudí Palace, Murcia, Spain.

Municipal Museum, Orense, Spain.

Rioja Cultural Center, Logroño, Spain.

1993 "Four Directions: Spanish Contemporary Photography 1970-90," Fine Arts Museum, Bilbao, Spain.

Palace of the Counts of Gavia, Granada.

BIBLIOGRAPHY

BOOKS

España oculta. Prologue by Julio Caro Baroja. Barcelona. Lunwerg Editores, 1989. 150 pp. (126 b/w photos).

Espagne occulte. Prologue by Claude Nori and Christian Caujolle. Paris. Contrejour, 1990. 152 pp. (126 b/w photos).

España oculta. Prologue by Julio Caro Baroja. Munich. Bucher, 1990. 156 pp. (126 b/w photos).

Europa: El sur. Introduction by Pablo López de Osaba. Prologue by Christian Caujolle. Madrid. Consorcio para la Organización de Madrid Capital Europea de la Cultura 1992. 128 pp. (100 b/w photos).

Spanien. Festes und Riten. Prologue by William A. Christian Jr. Text by Caballero Bonal. Schaffhausen. Stemmle, 1992. 291 pp. (187 colour photos).

España. Fiestas y Ritos. Prologue by William A. Christian Jr. Text by Caballero Bonal. Barcelona. Lunwerg, 1992. 273 pp. (187 colour photos).

Spagne. Feste e Riti. Prologue by William A. Christian Jr. Text by Caballero Bonal. Milan. Jaca Book, 1994. 291 pp. (187 colour photos).

BOOKS AND EXHIBITION CATALOGUES WHICH INCLUDE WORKS BY CRISTINA GARCIA RODERO

Everfoto. León. Everest, 1973.

Everfoto 2. León. Everest, 1974.

Otero Pedrayo, Ramón. *Galicia, una cultura de occidente*. León. Everest, 1975.

Everfoto 3. León. Everest, 1975.

II Exposición Becarios Artes Plásticas. Madrid. Fundación Juan March, 1976.

Everfoto 4. León. Everest, 1976.

Duran, José Antonio. *Galicia, realidad económica y conflicto social*. La Coruña. Banco de Bilbao, 1978.

Christian, Williams. *Local Religion in Sixteenth Century Spain*. Princeton. Princeton University Press, 1980.

259 Imágenes, fotografía actual en España. Madrid. Ministerio de Cultura, 1983.

Exposición de profesores en la Facultad de Bellas Artes. Madrid. Universidad Complutense, 1983.

Enciclopedia Planeta de la fotografía. Madrid. Planeta, 1984.

La fotografía en el museo. Madrid. Ministerio de Cultura, 1985.

Aspecten van Spanjen. Madrid. Europalia 85-España, 1985.

Foco 85. Fotografía contemporánea. Madrid. Círculo de Bellas Artes, 1985.

Photographies des practiques religeuses en pays méditerranéens. Journées Internationales de la Photographie. Montpellier, 1985.

Photografien Aus Spanien. Fotografische Sammlung. Essen. Museum Folkwang, 1985.

2.º Encuentro Fotográfico San Prudencio. Caja Provincial de Alava. Vitoria, 1986.

Hahn, Betty. *Contemporary Spanish Photography*. Albuquerque. University of New Mexico Press, 1987.

Galicia a pé de foto. Barcelona. Universidad Internacional Menéndez Pelayo/Lunwerg, 1987.

Un día en la vida de España. New York. Collins, 1987.

Cristina García Rodero. Vigo. Centro de Estudios Fotográficos. Consejería de Cultura, 1988.

Raíces judías en España. Madrid. Iberia, 1988.

Así es Madrid. Madrid. Temas de Hoy, 1988.

A Day in the Life of California. San Francisco. Collins, 1988.

Four Spanish Photographers. Prologue by James Enyeart. Text by Terrence Pitts. Tucson. Center for Creative Photography. University of Tucson, Arizona, 1988.

Soria, Castilla y León. Madrid. Mediterráneo, 1989.

Artistas españolas en Europa. Madrid. Ministerio de Cultura, 1989.

Ultimas miradas. Alhambra. Granada. Consejería de Cultura. Junta de Andalucía, 1990.

Le Méditerranée: La lumière eblouie. V Rencontres Photographiques. Carcassonne. G.R.A.P.H., 1990.

Valladolid, Castilla y León. Madrid. Mediterráneo, 1990.

Els paisatges de Joanot Martorell. Gandia i la Safor. Valencia. IVAM, Centre Julio González, 1990.

Vanishing Spain. New York. International Center of Photography, 1991.

Cuatro direcciones: Fotografía contemporánea española 1970-1990. Vol. I. Introduction by Manuel Santos. Barcelona. Lunwerg, 1991.

Méditerranéennes. Paris. Contrejour, 1991.

Aquí y ahora. Madrid. Consejería de Cultura. Comunidad de Madrid, 1991.

The Circle of Life. Pictures from the Human Family Album. Introduction by Gabriel García Márquez. San Francisco. Cohen, 1991.

Plenel, Edwy. *Voyage avec Colomb*. Le Monde, 1991.

Open Spain. Chicago. The Museum of Contemporary Photography. Barcelona. Lunwerg, 1992.

Astilleros del ayer al hoy. Introduction by Juan Sáez. Text by Fernando Quiñones. Barcelona. Lunwerg, 1992.

Papa, Cristina. *Il Pane*. Perugia. Electa, 1992.

I-D Nationale. Edinburgh. Portfolio Gallery, 1992.

García de León, María Antonia. *La ciudad contra el campo. Sociedad rural y cambio social*. Ciudad Real. Diputación de Ciudad Real, 1992.

W. Eugene Smith. Tokyo. Pacific Press Service, 1992.

Imagina. Un proyecto entorno a la fotografía. Almería. Almediterránea 92, 1992.

El Prado vivo. Madrid. Museo del Prado, 1992.

Plenel, Edwy. *Voyage avec Colom*. Tokyo. Shobun-sha, 1992.

Mora, Gilles. *L'Echappée européenne / Der Europaische Ausbruch*. Paris. Les Cahiers de la Photographie, 1992.

Homenaje a Gerardo Vielba. Madrid. Real Sociedad Fotográfica / "La Escuela de Madrid," 1993.

World Press Photo. London. Thames and Hudson, 1993.

PERIODICALS

Jorge Rueda. "Por el año internacional ese." *Nueva lente*, nos. 41-42. Madrid, July-August 1975, pp. 62-67. (5 photos and cover).

"España ritual." *Carta de España*, nos. 322-333. Madrid, 1986. (40 photos).

"A Day in the Life of California." *Hyatt Magazine*. Chicago, Autumn/Winter 1988, pp. 26-32. (1 photo).

"Fiesta! Spain Through a Camera." *Lookout*. Fuengirola, May 1989, pp. 48-55. (16 photos and cover).

María Angeles Sánchez. "España en negro." *El País semanal*, no. 631. Madrid, 21 May 1989, pp. 66-67. (14 photos).

Josef Oehrlein. "Kreuzweg." *Frankfurter Allgemeine Magazin*. Frankfurt, 8 September 1989, pp. 50-58. (8 photos).

Tim McGirk. "Mystic Spain." *The Independent Magazine*. London, 28 October 1989, pp. 46-54. (9 photos).

Alfonso M. Di Nola. "Dio è con noi." Giovanni Calvenzi. "A caccia di un'anima que scende dal cielo." *Corriere della sera*. Milan, 28 October 1989, pp. 46-77. (21 photos and cover).

"Cristina García Rodero. España oculta." *El Paseante*, no. 13. Madrid, 1989, pp. 62-71. (11 photos).

Cees Nooteboom. "Het Occulte Spanje." *Avenue*. Amsterdam, January 1990, pp. 86-91. (10 photos).

"Prières de L'Espagne secrète." *Geo*. Paris, January 1990, pp. 108-119. (13 photos).

Walter Tauber. "Wo Nur das Wellblech Glänzt." *Merian*, 3/XLIII. Hamburg, 1990, pp. 58-65. (8 photos).

Julio Caro Baroja. "La moda de España." *Marie Claire*, no. 30. Madrid, March 1990, pp. 10-19. (31 photos).

Piedad Moreno. "Locos: la vuelta a casa." *Marie Claire*, no. 30. Madrid, March 1990, pp. 69-74. (7 photos).

José Angel Valente. "Imágenes para una pasión." *Marie Claire*, no. 31. Madrid, April 1990, pp. 10-20. (12 photos).

Karl Steinorth. "Fotos des Glaubens." *Foto Magazin*, no. 5. Munich, May 1990, pp. 4, 26 and 29. (11 photos).

"Cristina García Rodero. Schwarzes Spanien." *Photo Technik International*. Munich, May-June 1990, pp. 74-81. (8 photos).

"Las fiestas de guardar." *Geo*, no. 41. Madrid, June 1990, pp. 86-87. (10 photos).

"Spanish Tradition." *Marie Claire*, no. 23. London, July 1990, pp. 10-17. (22 photos).

Mariàngels Farreny i Bordallo. "Einblicke in ein Wunderland." *Geo*, no. 9. Hamburg, September 1990, pp. 98-118. (16 photos).

Harald Irnberger. "Ein Andalusicher Hund." *Trans Atlantik*, no. 9. Hamburg, September 1990, pp. 37-42. (5 photos).

Igor Reyes-Ortiz. "El otro carnaval: Entrevista a Julio Caro Baroja." *Marie Claire*, no. 41. Madrid, February 1991, pp. 54-60. (21 photos).

Lobo. "Det Oculta Spanien." *Aktuell Fotografi*, no. 6. Helsingborg, 1991, pp. 44-49. (10 photos).

Consolación González Casarrubios. "Barroco español. Trajes populares."

Paisajes desde el tren, no. 5. Madrid, March 1991, pp. 50-59. (18 photos).

"Mil semanas que hacen historia 1971-1991." *Cambio 16*, no. 1000, pp. 251.

Various authors. "El mapa de España." *El País*. Madrid, 1-31 August 1991, (35 photos).

"Nonne el Gitane." *Vogue*, no. 722. Paris, December 1991-January 1992, pp. 292-299. (6 photos).

Vicky Hayward. "Women Bullfighters." *Marie Claire*, no. 43. London, March 1992, pp. 10-18. (13 photos).

Martin Symington. "Fiesta." *Telegraph Magazine*. London, 7 March 1992, pp. 24-34. (8 photos and cover).

Nathalie Dubois. "Le cœur catalan bat pour la communauté." *Libération*. Paris, 20 March 1992, pp. 23-25. (2 photos).

Jacques Maigne. "La vie de bric et de broc des gitans de Madrid." *Libération*. Paris, 20 March 1992, pp. 38.

"Ansicht." *Das Magazin*. 16/18 April 1992, pp. 26 and 27. (1 photo).

Jean Hébert Armengaud. "Expo'92. L'auberge espagnole." *Libération*. Paris, 21 March 1992, pp. 1-6. (6 photos and cover).

Javier Tomeo. "Ein Land Fuhrt Sich Auf." Munich, 30 April 1992, pp. 42-51. (9 photos).

"L'Espagne en fêtes." *Photo*, no. 293. Paris, April-May 1992, pp. 30-44. (23 photos).

Jacques Durand, Jacques Maigne and Patrick Sabatier. "Seville." *Libération*. Paris, 18 and 19 April 1992, pp. 17-24. (5 photos and cover).

Jacques Maigne. "Passion et délires des fêtes d'Espagne." *Geo*, no. 161. Paris, July 1992, pp. 26-39. (12 photos).

"Fiesta." *Marie Claire*. London, August 1992, pp. 10-21. (20 photos).

Tala Skari. "The Spectacle of Spain." *Life Magazine*. New York, August 1982, pp. 80-89. (11 photos).

Michel Bessières. "Fiestas d'Espagne. Dix siècles d'histoire dans la rue." *Le Figaro Magazine*. 5 September 1992, pp. 7, 64-71. (8 photos).

"Al rescate de las mayas." *La Capital*, no. 9. Madrid, September, 1992, pp. 24-25. (4 photos and cover).

"Retrato secreto. La España de Cristina García Rodero." *El País semanal*. Madrid, 15 November 1992, pp. 3, 82-90. (12 photos).

"Spanien...Fiert!" *Saison*. Hamburg, November and December 1992, pp. 4-7. (8 photos).

Julio Nombela. "El reinado de las máscaras." *Suplemento semanal*. Madrid, 27 December 1992, pp. 30-33. (8 photos).

"Ansicht." *Das Magazin*. Zurich, 10-13 March 1993, pp. 28-29. (1 photo).

Alan Weisman. "The Sacred and Profane." *Los Angeles Times Magazine*. Los Angeles, 11 April 1993, pp. 12-16. (8 photos and cover).

Louis Châtellier. "Mission en Espagne." *L'Histoire*, no. 163. February 1993, pp. 82-89. (6 photos).

"Big Pictures." *Spy*. New York, March 1993, pp. 66 and 67. (1 photo).

PUBLICATIONS ON CRISTINA GARCÍA RODERO

BOOKS AND CATALOGUES

Falces, Manuel. *Introducción a la fotografía española*. Granada. Universidad de Granada, 1975.

Sougez, Marie-Loup. *Historia de la fotografía*. Madrid. Cátedra, 1981.

Newhall, Beaumont. *Historia de la fotografía desde sus orígenes hasta nuestros días*. (Appendix on Spanish photography by Joan Fontcuberta). Barcelona. Gustavo Gili, 1983.

Provencio, Pedro. *Photographies des pratiques religieuses en pays méditerranéens*. Exhibition catalogue. Montpellier, 1985.

Verdugo, Oscar. *Foco-85*. Exhibition catalogue. Madrid. Cícrulo de Bellas Artes, 1985.

Yáñez Polo, Miguel Angel. Ortiz Lara,

Luis. Holgado Brenes, José Manuel. *Historia de la fotografía española 1839-1986*. Sociedad de Historia de la Fotografía Española. Seville, 1986.

Various authors. *La fotografía y sus posibilidades documentales. Una introducción a su utilización en las ciencias sociales*. Santander. Universidad de Cantabria, 1989.

Caro Baroja, Julio. Prologue to *España oculta*. Barcelona. Lunwerg, 1989.

Caujolle, Christian. Prologue to *Espagne occulte*. Paris. Contrejours, 1990.

Nori, Claude. "Le soleil des jours tristes de Houston." Text in *Espagne occulte*. Paris. Contrejours, 1990.

Colombo, Atilio. Presentation of the exhibition *España oculta* at the II Diaframma Gallery, Milan, 1990.

Mira, Enric. *La vanguardia fotográfica de los años 70 en España*. Alicante. Diputación Provincial de Alicante, 1991.

Santos, Manuel. *Cuatro direcciones. Fotografía contemporánea española, 1970-1990*. Vol II. Barcelona. Lunwerg, 1991.

Isler, Vera. *Rollenwechsel. Fotografen von der Kamera*. Kassel. Friedrich Reinhardt Verlag, 1992.

Caujolle, Christian. Presentation of *Europa: El sur*. Barcelona. Lunwerg/Consorcio para la Organización de Madrid Capital Europea de la Cultura, 1992.

Christian, William A. Jr. Presentation of *España. Fiestas y Ritos*. Barcelona. Lunwerg, 1992.

Caballero Bonald, José María. Foreword to *España. Fiestas y Ritos*. Barcelona. Lunwerg, 1992.

PERIODICALS

"Cristina García Rodero." *Revista de la Real Sociedad Fotográfica*. Madrid, November 1973, pp. 6-19. (12 photos).

Gerardo Vielva. "XVII Nacional Real Sociedad Fotográfica. Notas fotográficas madrileñas."

Revista de la Real Sociedad Fotográfica. Madrid, 1973.

Arte fotográfico. Madrid, November 1973, pp. 1419-1428. (1 photo).

"Cristina García Rodero: contra el tiempo." *Photo Español*, no. 47. London, 21 November 1980, pp. 1154-1157. (4 photos).

"13 fotógrafos contemporáneos españoles." *Poptografía*. Volume 2, no. 3. Madrid, March 1981, pp. 5-44. (3 photos).

Pedro Pardo. "Fotografías en el desván - Cristina García Rodero, una mujer sola." *El País semanal*, no. 380. Madrid, 1984 (1 photo).

Enrique Peral. "Cristina García Rodero, Premio Planeta de fotografía en su IV edición." *Arte fotográfico*, no. 399. Madrid, March 1985, pp. 271-280. (9 photos).

Rosa Olivares. "Las mil caras de la realidad." *Lápiz*, no. 26. Madrid, June 1985, pp. 24-30. (2 photos).

"Cristina García Rodero. Imágenes de la Premio Planeta de fotografía." *Foto profesional*, no. 27. Madrid, 1985, pp. 4-16. (20 photos).

"Cristina García Rodero y *su* tema: doce años de trabajo de investigación." *Internacional*, no. 3. November 1985, pp. 82-83. (1 photo).

"Tierras, gentes y ritos." *Photovisión*. Madrid, 1985. (10 photos).

Eduardo Momeñe. "El nuevo color: sus orígenes y antecedentes." *Photovisión*, no. 4. Madrid, 1985, pp. 10-47. (1 photo).

"Cristina García Rodero. Spain Through a Camera." *Lookout*. Fuengirola, February 1986, pp. 64-71. (10 photos).

Marta Riopérez. "Cristina García Rodero. Revelar España." *Elle*. Madrid, December 1988, p. 21. (1 photo).

"A Day in the Life of California." *Hyatt Magazine*. Chicago, Autumn/Winter 1988, pp. 26-32. (1 photo).

José María Plaza. "Galería de fotógrafos españoles. Cristina García Rodero." *Diario 16 semanal*, no. 383. Madrid, 29 January 1989, p. 58. (1 photo).

Guillermo Mañares. "Cien castellano-manchegos. Cristina García Rodero." *Revista de Información de la Junta de Comunidades, Castilla-La Mancha*. Toledo, May 1989, p. 39.

"Ritualen." *Volkskrant*. 3 June 1989, p. 11 (8 photos).

Pedro Madueño. "Imágenes que valen más que mil palabras." *La Vanguardia*. Barcelona, 30 July 1989.

Gabriel Bauret. "Humain, très humain." *Photographies Magazine*. Paris, Summer 1989, pp. 68-81. (4 photos).

Lourdes Berraondo. "Cristina García Rodero: voluntad a prueba." *Foto profesional*, no. 8. August 1989, pp. 27-35. (8 photos).

José María Bermejo. "La España oculta en 126 imágenes." *El Independiente*. Madrid, 15 August 1989, p. 24. (3 photos).

José María Fernández. "España oculta. Lo ancestral al descubierto." *Reseña*, no. 198. Madrid, September 1989, p. 24. (3 photos).

Luis Alonso Fernández. "La mirada viajera." *Reseña*, no. 198. Madrid, September 1989, p. 48. (1 photo).

Antonio Molinero. "España en blanco y negro." *FV*, no. 15. Madrid, 1989, pp. 70-71. (1 photo).

Maite Alfajeme. "Desde su punto de vista. Hablan 5 prestigiosas fotógrafas." *Epoca*, no. 253. Madrid, 12 January 1990, pp. 59-63. (1 photo).

Gerardo Vielva. "Cristina García Rodero. Un realismo trascendido." *La Fotografía*, no. 9. Barcelona, January 1990, pp. 30-37. (7 photos).

Carole Naggar. "The Disguised Spirit of Spain." *Camera International*, no. 4. New York, Winter 1990, pp. 20-85. (2 photos).

Dolors Pérez. "Fotógrafas de sí mismas (Cristina García Rodero, pasión)." *La Vanguardia Magazine*. Barcelona, 15 April 1990, p. 86.

Giovanna Calvenzi. "Cámara oscura." *Vogue*, no. 25. Madrid, April 1990, pp. 106-109. (5 photos).

"Prix Erich Salomon, Cristina García Rodero, España oculta." *Leica Fotografie Internacional*. April 1990, pp. 10-15. (9 photos).

"Espagne occulte par Cristina García Rodero." *Photo Magazine*. June 1990, p. 18. (1 photo).

Emma Dent Coad. "Women of La Mancha. The Reportage Photography of C.G.R." *British Journal of Photography*, no. 6782. London, August 1990, pp. 16-19. (4 photos and cover).

Leigh Hatts. "España viva in Black and White." *Catholic Herald*, 3 August 1990.

Andrew Palmer. "Shot from Within." *The Independent*. London, 23 August 1990. (1 photo).

Denis Curti. "Riti e misteri di Spagna." *Vivimilano*. 6 September 1990.

Roberto Mutti. "Arriva la Spagna di Hemingway." *Tuttomilano*. Milan, 6 September 1990.

Lanfranco Colombo. "In Galleria." *Foto Prattica*. Milan, September 1990, p. 76.

"Exhibition." *International Center of Photography 1991 Annual Report*. New York, 1991, pp. 22-39. (2 photos).

"Diez maestros de la cámara eligen *mi foto preferida*." *Muy Especial*, no. 8. Madrid, Winter 1992, pp. 16-17. (1 photo).

Juan Ignacio Fernández. "En busca del alma dormida." *El Correo Español, El Pueblo Vasco (extra domingo)*. Bilbao, 16 February 1992, pp. 14-15. (6 photos).

Xavier Martí. "Visa pour l'image. IV Festival Internacional de Fotoreportaje." *La Fotogafía*, no. 30. Barcelona, 1992, pp. 5-21. (2 photos).

Carol Squiers. "The Europeans." *American Photo*. New York. March/April 1992, pp. 45-71. (1 photo).

Xosé Manuel Rodríguez. "España oculta, lección de antropología." *La Voz de Galicia*. 30 April 1992.

Judith Russi Kirshner. "People and Ideas. Post-Franco Modernism." *Aperture*, no. 127. New York, Spring 1992, pp. 72-73. (1 photo).

Percy Hopewell. "La España de Cristina García Rodero." *Suplemento semanal*, no. 238. Madrid, 17 May 1992, pp. 26-32. (5 photos).

Gabriel Bauret. "Les Editions Lunwerg." *Photographies Magazine*, no. 41. Paris, May 1992, p. 35.

Rafael Levenfeld. "Une histoire hypothétique, l'alliance des matériaux." *Photographies Magazine*, no. 41. Paris, May 1992, pp. 66-73. (1 photo).

Antonio Arco. "Fotografías que sí hablan." *La Verdad*. Saturday, 12 June 1992, p. 41. (4 photos).

Nane L'Hostis. "Scoop toujours!" *Télérama*. 29 August 1992, pp. 16-18. (1 photo).

J.E. "Viaje al corazón de un país." *Diario de Navarra*. Pamplona, 13 September 1992, p. 45. (4 photos).

Feliciano López Pastor. "Cristina García Rodero." *La Fotografía*, no. 31. Barcelona, October 1992, pp. 49-53. (8 photos).

Patricio Salinas. "Spanska Ritualer." *F / Fotografisk Tidskrift*, no. 4. Stockholm, 1992, pp. 34-39. (7 photos).

"Nachschlag." *Der Feinschmecker*. Hamburg, June 1993, pp. 128 and 129.

Reijo Rinnekangas. "Cristina García Rodero." *Image*. Helsinki, Feburary, 1993, pp. 67-81. (22 photos).

Rosa Valdelomar. "La fiesta es una excusa para estudiar el comportamiento humano." *ABC*. Madrid, 19 November 1993, p. 60.

Andrés F. Rubio. "García Rodero desvela en imágenes el choque entre lo viejo y lo nuevo." *El País*. Madrid, 19 November 1993, p. 33. (1 photo).

Manuel Falces. "Tópicos hechos documentos." *El País*. Madrid, 22 November 1993, p. 26.

Javier López Rejas. "Un paseo por la fiesta y la muerte." *Diario 16*. Madrid, 30 November 1993, pp. 8 and 9. (4 photos).

INDEX